SCRIPTLESSNESS

A Missing Dimension in Zero-to-Hero Tales

By

Benjamin Addai Antwi-Boasiako

Dedication

I dedicate this book to all beset by experiences too delicate to be voiced.

Preface

Imagine a desert plant whose roots run deep in the sands of the Sahara. If you uproot it and plant it in the Amazon forest, the new soil will surely be rich, but that doesn't mean the plant will thrive since it's so far removed from the conditions that once nurtured it.

People aren't so different. If you grow up in a poor, rural home and climb out of poverty, the world you step into might have opportunities, but you might find it overwhelming. Our upbringing shapes our habits and how we see the world. So, when things change suddenly, it can feel like being tossed into deep waters without a life vest.

Scriptlessness sheds light on the struggles no one talks about when success comes out of nowhere, the awkwardness of suddenly being in a different social class, the guilt that can come with success, and the unsettling feeling of being a stranger in both the world you once knew and your current circles.

B. Addai Antwi-Boasiako

Taufkirchen am Wald, 20 April 2025

Contents

Prologue

Life gives what you sacrifice

I was *likely* born in 1979. After many years of political upheaval and economic downturn, Ghana stood at a critical juncture. Dr. Hilla Limann had been elected president, and the country wavered between hope and despair. The scars of instability ran deep. The harsh realities of daily life were evident, with essential commodities like fuel being scarce.

But the hardship peaked in the hinterlands, far from the urban centres. Poor road networks left rural areas isolated. Against this backdrop, a pregnant lady, Margaret, travelled about 150 kilometres to join her husband at his cocoa farm cottage.

However, part of the road connecting the two regions was in shambles after many years of neglect. The wooden truck that Margaret and other passengers boarded couldn't reach their destination, leaving them stranded. From there, they had to make the remaining 20 kilometres on foot. This daunting task was even more difficult for Margaret as she had a one-year-old.

The toll this taxing trek took on her was evident in the following weeks. She was physically paralysed, barely able to stand, let alone walk. It was during this immobilised state that she went into labour on a Saturday in a storeroom in the farm cottage, where she had dragged herself to break palm kernels.

Going to a clinic wasn't an option because that would've required them to use a cloth to create a makeshift stretcher by fastening its ends to two poles. She would then lie on this stretcher, and four people would carry her on their shoulders to walk long distances to reach the nearest healthcare centre. Given the circumstances, they called a traditional birth attendant to help her give birth in the cottage.

Despite the diligent efforts of the attendant and the passing of more than 24 hours, Margaret couldn't give birth. They tried various traditional remedies, giving her herbal decoctions to speed up the process, but all proved futile. Hours morphed into days, with Sunday and Monday slipping by without progress. Growing ever more alarmed about the potential risk to her life, the attendant had to prioritise her well-being. It was more prudent to save her life, even if it meant losing the child. They backed this decision with an Akan proverb: *It is better for the water to pour away than for the water pot to break.*

Yet, against all odds, Margaret gave birth to a baby boy on a Tuesday after yet another round of herbal remedies.

Margaret and her newborn – the water and the water pot – survived. That newborn, the water within the pot, was me.

That humble farm cottage, aptly named emere-dane (times change), was where I entered the world. Perhaps it's the near tragedy that led my parents to name me Benjamin, drawing parallels to the Biblical story where Rachel died while giving life to her son, Benjamin. But that is only a guess.

The mystery of my first name isn't the only puzzle in my life. Even my date of birth is shrouded in uncertainty. That's why I began that my birth year was *likely* 1979, a tentative claim rooted in the absence of formal records. My parents, loaded by the pressures of my birth, didn't register my birth. The nearest registry was a distance away. They had other priorities, given the conditions of my birth.

It was about the cusp of my teenage years that I asked my father about my birth date. He quickly recalled that I was born on the 2nd of October. Somehow, he couldn't remember the year. With this information, I started a search to pinpoint my birth year. I thought that if I could identify a year in which the 2nd of October fell on a Tuesday,* I might finally unravel the mystery of my birth date.

---

* In Ghana, the Akan people name their children based on the day of the week they were born. Each day of the week corresponds to a specific name for both males and females. For example, a male born on Tuesday is named *Kwabena*, while a

3

This task, however, proved trickier than I thought, as calendars from the 1970s and early 1980s weren't readily available then. Could the first school I attended provide a clue? Regrettably, no. The date recorded by the school was a guess, as I explain next.

Tricked by the prospects of food

In 1983, when I was about four, bushfires swept through Ghana and razed down the cocoa farm that was my father's pride. At the outset of the fires, my mother whisked us away from the farm cottage to Kuntunso, a village with some 50 homes, about 150 kilometres from my place of birth. It's at Kuntunso that my schooling began – in unusual circumstances.

One day, my sister, Susan, went to school and left a book at home. My mother asked me to deliver it to her. When I arrived at the school, I saw traditional three-rock cookstoves under a shade tree. As a result of the famine that the 1983 droughts and fires brought, this scene made me curious. Could it be that they served meals to the pupils and nobody told me? I decided, at once, that I would attend school.

I came home and told my mother about my decision. She advised that I wait until the end of the school year, but I was determined. If my mother thought I was joking, my early

---

female is named *Abena*. Similarly, a male born on Friday is named *Kofi*, and a female is named *Afia*.

4

rise the following day showed her that my resolve was resolute. My siblings were embarrassed by my antics and refused to let me go with them to school, so I set off alone in casual attire.

Even though I initially went to the wrong class, Madam *Bee* (Beatrice), the class one teacher, warmly welcomed me. It helped that my elder brother, Nana, was one of the brightest pupils in the school. My name wasn't in the class register, but it didn't bother me. However, my initial hope – that they gave meals to the pupils – was dashed when I found out that the food was meant for adults engaged in communal labour at the school. That notwithstanding, I decided to keep on. Given how I had insisted, I had no choice.

I attended school until the vacation period arrived, a span that felt both brief and endless. Madam Bee asked me to remain in her class at the beginning of the new term, even as my erstwhile classmates advanced to class two. She assigned me a birth date. When new pupils arrived in class one, my familiarity with the environment gave me a head start. Madam Bee made me the class captain.

I enjoyed schooling for another, *hidden* reason. Growing up in the village, people made cruel comments about the shape of my head. So, when I began schooling and excelled in my studies, school became my sanctuary, where I could show my brilliance. Good grades seemed a rebellion against the cruel remarks about my head.

Two years in the wilderness

After completing class four, I went, as usual, to my birthplace, my father's cottage, during the long vacation. My father had started replanting his burnt cocoa farm, and my mother had returned, leaving us in the care of our grandmother. We usually spent our days on the farm from Monday to Saturday during the vacation. I hated the daily routine of going to the farm. I asked my father to assign me a specific portion of the farm to weed during the vacation period. Once I finish this contract, my time will be my own. He agreed. Driven by the desire for freedom, I would rise early and work late, allowing me to complete my tasks in a week.

I used my free time to hunt birds. I enjoyed entering the forest. During one such expedition, I suffered a severe leg injury. It forced me to remain at the cottage beyond the vacation period. When my leg finally healed, I told my father, much to my mother's chagrin, that I wanted to attend school in the village. My mother didn't want me to attend school there, fearing it would affect me. The six-kilometre trek through the forest from the farm cottage to Kwasarekrom Catholic Primary School didn't deter me. Was I running away from those hurtful comments about the shape of my head?

I enrolled in the village school in class five. It quickly became clear that I was in a league of my own. I was the only student who could write an essay about myself. I was the village champion. By the end of the school year, the authorities proposed that I skip the sixth grade and go directly to the seventh (the first year of junior secondary). It was hardly surprising, given that the pupils who had schooled there all their lives spent more time working on teachers' farms than they did in actual studies. I enjoyed my days in the farm cottage until I was forced to leave the school.

Blessing in disguise

One afternoon after school, a friend, Kwaku, asked me to help him write a love letter to Emelia, a beautiful girl in our class. I obliged. I wrote his heartfelt words. Kwaku's joy was noticeable as I read aloud the letter I had written. I guess he never slept that night.

The following morning, Kwaku was the first to arrive at school, ready to give the letter to Emelia. But his hopes were dashed. Emelia got angry after reading the letter and reported the matter to the authorities. The headteacher and Emelia agreed that Kwaku couldn't have written the letter, and the handwriting was mine. When they asked, he admitted that I had written the letter for him.

Unaware of the mess the letter had caused, I was summoned alongside Kwaku during the usual morning assembly. As I stood before the assembled school, memories of my past mischiefs crept into my mind, and then I remembered the letter.

My fears were confirmed when the teacher told the school that we, pre-teens, had written a romantic letter to Emelia, making *wild* promises. I insisted on my innocence. The teacher would have none of that, citing a proverb: *The lizard says it does not find the person who threw a stone at it as annoying as the one who praised his marksmanship.* To the teacher, I was the spider at the centre of the ugly web. Our punishment? We were to lie on a table and receive lashes. I vowed not to take the canes, and it marked my last day at the school.

When I returned home, I told my mother I no longer wished to attend the village school because we spent too much time working on our teachers' farms (you didn't expect me to tell the truth, did you?). She was pleased that I had finally seen reason since she had always opposed my schooling in the village. She promised to send me to Techiman to continue my education.

About a week before the love letter case, I had run into an older woman struggling to carry a bundle of firewood. I offered to help, and she was deeply grateful. When we reached her home, she *blessed* me, and I felt her words would come true. So, when the love letter incident happened, I was dismayed to find myself in such a mess shortly after her blessing. But in hindsight, I realised I needed that to leave the village school. Had that embarrassing incident not occurred, I might have remained in the village and never gone beyond junior secondary school.

A small fish in a big pond

My move from the farm cottage to the urban settings of Techiman was my first real shock. Initially, finding a school in Techiman proved challenging, with multiple rejections. My mother eventually gave up and returned to the farm cottage, leaving me with a distant aunt I had never met. I helped my aunt and her husband at their grocery shop, assuming my education was over. However, my uncle noticed my reading habits (even with foreign newspapers) and promised to find a school for me.

We visited several schools, facing rejection until we arrived at the Seventh Day Adventist Junior Secondary School. The assistant headteacher accepted me, allowing me to start school the next day. Despite struggling initially, I improved after two terms of hard work. Yet, the Basic Education Certificate Examination came too early for me. My results were average.

Convinced that I wasn't academically good enough, my father suggested I become an electrician, which I reluctantly agreed to. But my mother noticed I wasn't happy and asked what was bothering me. I told her I would love to continue my studies. She agreed and enrolled me in Techiman

Secondary School, defying my father. I was determined to succeed and earned a merit scholarship by the end of my first year. It allowed me to become a boarding student in my second year.

During high school, I found that my probable birth date was 2 October 1979 (a Tuesday). Despite some doubts, I used this date to get my first birth certificate.

It was during my final year that I used something as common as a water closet for the first time. This meeting came during a school trip to Sekondi-Takoradi, where I found myself in a mess at Fijai Senior High School's restroom. After attending nature's call, I didn't know how to dispose of the waste. Faced with the dilemma of not wanting to leave an unpleasant surprise for the next person, I tried various methods to no avail. Finally, I resorted to pulling on a handle.

Suddenly, water started gushing out. I stood there, watching in horror as the water level in the bowl rose like a tsunami. It was a battle of wits between me and the toilet bowl! *Calm down, toilet,* I tried to reason as if it would heed my plea. But no, it seemed resolute to flood the entire floor, or so I feared. When I braced myself for the worst, the water decided it had better things to do than drown me. It kindly vanished into the mysterious plumbing abyss. The relief that washed over me felt like I were Atlas, and the heavy burden of the sky had been lifted from my shoulders.

It was also a relief that I excelled in my Senior Secondary School Exams. However, there was a two-year waiting period for entry to university due to a backlog caused by a university teachers' strike.

Unwilling to go to the village for two years, I considered Technical Universities (then called Polytechnics), which offered Higher National Diplomas (which we were told were equivalent to degrees). I applied to Kumasi Technical University. When my name was missing from the admission list, I enquired. The then Head of the Department, Mr. Amoako Atta, revealed that my grades were too good, and they assumed I would leave for university, occupying a spot that could benefit another candidate. I assured him of my desire to complete the programme, and he prepared an admission letter for me.

While at Kumasi, I visited Accra, Ghana's capital, for the first time. The city's busyness, especially in an election year, exhausted me. I wondered if I could survive its buzz, let alone call it home.

The changing climate

After my studies at Kumasi Technical University, I did my mandatory national service at Sunyani Technical University. I lived in a single room in a bungalow on campus. It was my very first private room.

Amid this new freedom, a worrying thought began to gnaw at my mind. What if this freedom led me down a path of poor choices, especially given my acquaintances with many young women there? The privacy, I feared, could easily lead to recklessness. To counter this, I decided to *tie myself to the mast*, so to speak, by inviting a guy to share my room and serve as a moral compass.

After two years, I moved to a new job in insurance to fulfil a dream inspired by the loss of my father's cocoa plantation in 1983. Towards the end of my national service, I sent unsolicited applications to every insurance company in Ghana. Despite a mistake in the address, Vanguard Assurance received my letter and offered me a job. In my time with Vanguard, I chartered as an Insurer with the Chartered Insurance Institute, London. I also graduated from the Cape Coast University.

It was in Sunyani that I used the liff for the first time. The Cocoa House, the tallest building in town, was the sole possessor of a lift. Even in my early 20s, I saw the lift as a puzzling device to avoid. I fed myself a sour-grape narrative: "It's healthier to take the stairs." Yet, on one hot afternoon, when my colleague Angie invited me to join her in the lift, I seized the opportunity to watch, with a furtive glance, how she operated this mechanical wonder.

As Angie pressed the buttons and the lift doors closed, I felt a surge of confidence. It seemed more straightforward than I had imagined. However, the ride proved to be a lasting experience. My knees wobbled like those of a newborn giraffe. My chest heaved, each breath a frantic grasp for the sweet release of open air, as if I had emerged from the depths of a suffocating abyss, clawing urgently for daylight. Yet, outwardly, I kept a veneer of calm, never ready to betray myself.

After six years in Sunyani, I was transferred to Accra, something I dreaded. Despite Abel (who served as my moral compass in Sunyani) offering me a place to stay temporarily and guiding me, I found Accra's busy life overwhelming. I would later join another insurance company, Activa. There, I had the chance to attend a workshop on crop insurance organised by the German International Development Cooperation Agency (GIZ). I later joined a committee to design an index-based crop insurance product.

This involvement sparked an interest in climate change. I thought that with climate change, terrible events like the 1983 droughts and fires could become more frequent. I believed the insurance sector could help in climate change adaptation and wanted to learn more. My search led me to Potsdam University in Germany, where a master's course in public management offered a unique focus on integrating environmental challenges into political and administrative decision-making. I applied and was accepted into a scholarship programme with the German Academic Service Exchange (DAAD).

When my EgyptAir flight landed at Frankfurt Airport on 1 April 2012, it was hard to believe I had arrived in Germany. Was it a dream or an April Fool's prank? The crisp spring air quickly confirmed my reality. After passport control and collecting my luggage, I couldn't help but note the orderliness, a big change from the chaos at Kotoka Airport in Accra a day earlier.

I needed a luggage trolley, but they were chained and required a coin to unlock. Unaware that returning the trolley would refund the coin, I left it at the train platform, thinking the fee was for the service.

My next journey was to Dresden, where I was due to learn German for six months before starting my master's course. My train ticket showed an 11:04 departure, which I interpreted in the Ghanaian manner as a window between 11:00 and 11:15. I was amazed when the train arrived at 11:02 and left precisely at 11:04. Amazing!

While on the train, I watched the German landscape roll by. Green fields, quaint villages, graffiti-covered walls, and unique architecture created a charming scene. It was a perfect scene to reflect on my move to Germany. It was a leap of faith, but it felt right. After the language course, I moved to Potsdam for my master's course.

Staying in Germany

After graduating, I wanted to extend my stay in Germany. Yet, with limited German language skills, I knew finding a job would be difficult. So, I sought a PhD opportunity to extend my stay in Germany. Luckily, I got one in Dresden, the city that first welcomed me to Germany. I was thrilled at the prospect of three more years in Germany. After three challenging years, I submitted my dissertation.

Again, I wanted to remain in Germany. Even before defending my thesis, I decided to explore my options. I thought of Susan Gille, the Project Manager I worked with on the GIZ insurance project in Ghana. She had returned to GIZ's head office in Germany. I sent her my resume, which she shared with her contacts. This set off a series of events that changed my life.

One contact shared my CV with my future boss, who contacted me about an opening they had. I applied. After a rigorous process, I received a permanent job offer. It offered a realistic path to stay in Germany. After joining the company, though, the luxury overwhelmed me. It was a dream come true, but it stirred mixed emotions. I doubted if I deserved such a position.

1: The sky off my shoulders

In Greek mythology, Atlas had the burden of carrying the sky on his shoulders for eternity. After years of bearing the weight, Heracles came across him. Heracles needed Atlas' help to fetch some apples, so he offered to take the sky off Atlas' shoulders briefly. When he took on the weight of the sky, he staggered, unable to stay steady.

When we hear this story, it's easy to focus on how tough it must have been for Heracles to carry the sky. We might also think Atlas was relieved to get a break, even if just for a moment. But let's think about it a bit differently. Imagine the toll the weight must have taken on Atlas over the years: his muscles, his bones, his whole body shaped by that burden. And then (boom!) the sky's off his shoulders.

It might seem like a relief, but it could also leave him unsteady, disoriented. To hurriedly get rid of a burden you've carried for long can be as unsettling as bearing it. But who's going to listen to Atlas's side of things? After all, the sky off his shoulders is good!

Now, imagine you fall from wealth to poverty (I hope not!). It's easy to share your struggles. Like Heracles, your pain is obvious; many will listen and offer support when you tell your story.

But what about if you leap from empty to plenty? We'll celebrate your success, even envy you. But, like Atlas, how do you adjust to your new reality? And who's going to listen to your story? Since we see escaping poverty as a blessing, if you tell others about your struggles *after* success, they might not listen and even see you as an ingrate. You've got what others are praying for, and you still complain? Thus, it's safer to stay silent.

But that silence has a price. If you don't speak up, those struggles stay bottled up. Ultimately, you're left feeling confused and without a *script* for how to deal with it. Society has guides for handling many situations but not for dealing with the loss of direction that comes with sudden success. Psychologist Baumeister and others call this *scriptlessness*; it's the feeling of having no guide to follow when you find yourself in unfamiliar territory.

Sleeping on a Procrustean bed

As I showed in the prologue, life was simple and unadorned in the Ghanaian farm cottage where I was born. Situated amid a cocoa farm bordered by rainforest, the cottage was a world unto itself with only two houses. The occasional, uninvited visits of scorpions, frogs, marauding army ants, snakes, or other unfriendly animals dotted the nights. Sporadic sounds of hunters' gunshots and eerie cries of tree hyraxes filled the night air.

The nearest village, Kwasarekrom, with a modest population of about 400 people, was about six kilometres away. Even there, cars were rare, and hitching a ride in the trucks that came to cart cocoa beans was a dreamy experience. Goats, sheep, and pigs roamed freely, sharing the open spaces with us.

The simplicity of that rural life is now a distant memory. I live in Munich, a city of about 1.5 million people, and work for a prestigious multinational company. This rise comes with the frills of success: business-class flights, nights in opulent hotels, and dinners at the finest restaurants. Meanwhile, not long ago, a sardine meal was a rare treat.

It's not all roses, though. My rise has put me on a Procrustean bed, a distressful place where I'm too short or too long, forever out of sync with its demands. The world of my corporate life is as alien to my illiterate parents as their cocoa farm is to my work colleagues. Moving from a blue-collar home to a white-collar job, from rural life to urban complexity, from illiteracy to earning a PhD, and from poverty to financial stability has thrust me into a world I never prepared for – socially, culturally, mentally.

Yet, we rarely discuss the cost of rapid upward social mobility. Most zero-to-hero tales paint an overly optimistic picture. Indeed, a co-worker, after hearing my story, suggested I write a book, likening me to a modern-day Ragged Dick. Even though I found the idea of writing a book to share my story enticing, it gave me a dilemma: How could I write to inspire others when I know that my story doesn't end in the usual "and he lived happily ever after"? So, I decided to turn the zero-to-hero trope on its head and shed light on the missing dimension of such tales.

The missing dimension

You probably get the idea that moving from Ghana to Germany (*geographic migration*) comes with acculturative stress. The new and different weather, language, food, and way of life can be overwhelming. However, with geographic migration, most people recognise the struggle. So, it's easy to find support, whether venting about the weather on social media or getting help translating a letter. Several guidebooks exist advising on how to *survive* in a new country.

So, this personal essay transcends the challenges of geographic migration. Moving from a poor, rural, illiterate home to a high-paying job in the city after earning a doctorate is also a kind of migration, even if it occurs in the same country. Some call it *class migration.* It's a messy mix of financial, social, and emotional challenges. You're stuck in between, unsure how much of this new world you should embrace so you don't lose your identity. There are hardly any books advising how to survive in this new *world.*

Those who tell their rags-to-riches stories often focus on their struggles *before* success. This approach makes it seem like everything is smooth sailing once you escape poverty.

While those stories tap into our innate optimism and are uplifting, reality doesn't care about narrative tropes. In the real world, sudden success often comes with stress, pressure, anxiety, and loneliness.

The ancients knew this. In Ghana, for example, the Akans have a saying: *If you try to whiten your teeth overnight, it leaves you with bleeding gums.* The philosopher Edmund Burke warned about the same thing when discussing the French Revolution: too much change, too soon, can lead to chaos. He echoed insight from Ancient Greece, as the following story about Paris of Troy shows.

From Mount Ida to Trojan Palace

A dark prophecy overshadowed the joy of King Priam and Queen Hecuba of Troy at the birth of their second son. It foretold that the new baby would destroy Troy. To thwart fate, the couple handed over the infant to a herder to end his life. But the herder, moved by the child's beauty, couldn't. He secretly raised him as Paris on Mount Ida and lied to the royal couple that their son was dead.

On his eighteenth birthday and still unaware of his royal lineage, Paris went to Troy to take part in the annual funeral games held in memory of his supposed death. He won easily. But the victory of such a yokel angered a royal. It led to a confrontation, out of which the truth of Paris' identity came out.

The herder confessed Paris's identity, and Priam and Hecuba embraced him as their son and prince. They reasoned that if Paris had lived eighteen years and Troy remained intact, then the prophecy was flawed. The royal family rejoiced, and Paris was welcomed to the palace.

Learning how to act royal

What a remarkable turnaround. Waking up as a shepherd on the slopes of Mount Ida, Paris could hardly have imagined the fantastic turn his life would take by the day's end. Yet, from tending his flock, he was thrust into the luxury of princely life. But the sudden change wasn't all roses.

For sure, Paris would've found life as a prince more pleasant. He had riches, fine clothes, food, and drinks. Yet, given his nurture and lack of exposure, Paris had to pay a price for his new status. He had to know many things and *act royal.* As Stephen Fry notes in his book *Troy,* "Paris was a born athlete… But now he was expected to translate his natural athleticism into the harder skills of soldiering. Unlike his brothers, he did not have the muscular strength and military discipline required of a warrior."

His struggles went beyond the arts of war. He found the arts of peace also tedious. For someone used to chasing calves, lambs, kids, and piglets, how could he know and discuss history, diplomacy, protocol, law, and taxation? What did they even mean?

Growing up on the slopes of Mount Ida, Paris learned the suitable scripts for Mount Ida. Thus, when he sneaked into Troy on the morning of his eighteenth birthday to take part in the funeral games, it wasn't only the city's grandeur that left him awed. He was also unsure about how to take part in the games. He was uncertain of the next steps after asking and receiving directions to join a line of youth in front of a table.

When the king and the queen came to the city's main gate to officially open the games, all the contestants promptly fell to their knees. Paris realised that he was the only one still standing. During the king's speech, the athletes beat their chests, shouting, "Strong! Fair! Proud! Trojan!" Initially, Paris didn't join in because he had no idea what to say. The other athletes knew the scripts – the sequence of events to follow. Paris didn't.

A gradual ascent would have allowed him to inertly pick up essential skills, scripts, values and tastes through socialisation and cultural exposure. His sudden change required him to adjust to new norms, behaviours, and scripts. When you make such a move, verbal or non-verbal cues or stereotypes can pressure you to conform to your new class's standards. Resisting such pressures is costly.

Running before learning to crawl

Understanding why Paris struggled to fit into his new, better world may be helpful. Change can manifest in two distinct ways: it can be gradual, unfolding gently over time, or it can be abrupt, arriving with a sudden jolt. Gradual changes, such as football players engaging in a warm-up routine before a match, allow them to gradually prepare their bodies, elevate their heart rates, and improve blood circulation. This process loosens their joints, enhances blood flow, and helps them mentally prepare for the game.

Conversely, abrupt changes can be disorienting, and we're poorly equipped to manage them. Psychologists like Kurt Lewin have developed a framework to help us understand our responses to change, often depicted through comfort, growth, and panic zones (*Figure 1*).

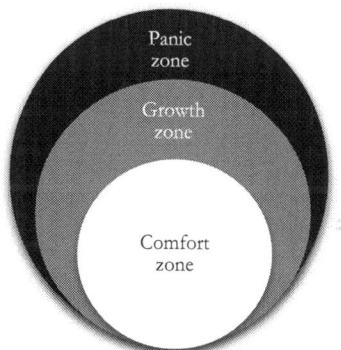

Figure 1: Zone Growth Model Concept

Your comfort zone consists of situations which look familiar to you, where you feel secure, at ease, in control. The growth zone is where you face new challenges, pushing the boundaries of your current abilities. Finally, the panic zone is a state of great stress and anxiety, where the changes you face seem unbeatable, and your ability to cope is severely compromised.

For Paris, his abrupt change thrust him out of his comfort zone, bypassed the growth zone, and into the panic zone. Such a leap left no room to adjust gradually. In Germany, educators understand this. They use a concept called *Eingewöhnungphase* to ease kids' transition from home to kindergarten. This term roughly translates as *the settling-in phase.* It's a structured approach to help kids adjust to their new peers, environment, and educators. At the outset, a parent goes with the child to the care centre for a specified period, slowly allowing the child to adapt to the staff and new surroundings.

Johny Just Come (JJC)

It'll be helpful to settle on a name for those who move from empty to plenty. Two terms come to mind: *class migrant* and *Johnny Just Come (JJC)*. A *class migrant* is a person who moves from one class to another, either climbing up or falling down the class ladder. But for this discussion, we only talk about those who move *up* quickly.

That said, I'll mostly use *JJC.* This term takes me back to my secondary school days in Ghana, where most students lived in boarding houses. First-year boarders went through an informal initiation to help them adjust. Those who transferred into boarding life later, having started the first year as day students, missed that process. They were branded

JJCs. It meant they were unfamiliar with the system's unspoken rules.

If you're a class migrant, you're a JJC in your new social class. You've entered a world where the old rules you grew up with don't fit. The people around you seem to steer everything effortlessly, but you're stuck trying to decode silent cues and hidden expectations. It's a world where everyone else seems to *know* how things work, leaving you feeling out of place and unsure of yourself.

I've gone through many transitions: rural to urban, blue-collar to white-collar, illiteracy to a doctorate, Ghana to Germany. Thus, my intersected experiences as a JJC might not match someone else's. Besides, we have different levels of cultural sensitivity. So, I won't pretend my story represents *every* class migrant's journey. But I believe many of the challenges I've faced aren't just personal quirks or bad luck; they are tied to deeper, structural issues that affect many JJCs.

Let me hasten to clarify that this book is not a memoir. Instead, it's a personal essay with a simple message: How you're raised shapes your habits, and those habits shape how you see and respond to the world. If the world you live in as an adult differs drastically from the one you grew up in, those old habits might not serve you anymore. In fact, they can hold you back.

2: Lonely in a crowded room

In his memoir, *My First Coup D'état*, Ghanaian President John Mahama tells the tale of Ezra, a young boy who, in the mid-1960s, attended Achimota School, one of Ghana's elite pre-tertiary institutions. Ezra, an illiterate cocoa farmer's son, joined Achimota at around ten. His father had good intentions for his son. But he quickly replaced his familiar routine of hunting birds in the forest with the new experience of mingling with the children of Ghana's elite. Mahama, whose father was a Member of Ghana's Parliament, recalls that Ezra had difficulties fitting in.

In explaining Ezra's struggles, Mahama's words betray a certain disdain, laced with stereotypical assumptions. "I was not at all surprised to learn that his father was a farmer," Mahama writes, "though I would have guessed it was an animal farm and not a cocoa farm, for Ezra looked as though he had been born, raised, and fed much like livestock... Ezra was a bush boy; he was tactless and uncouth."

Mahama and his peers were mainly the children of accountants, architects, bankers, chemists, doctors, engineers, insurers, judges, lawyers, politicians. They had been together in the boarding house since age six and shared a common social class origin. They knew how to make a telephone call, used a library, had parents who could afford trips abroad, and were used to reading newspapers.

That contrasted starkly with Ezra's background. It's likely that before attending Achimota, Ezra didn't know how to switch off lights or use a water closet. He couldn't speak a word of English. None of his new peers shared his expertise in poaching rats, setting traps, hunting birds, or working on a cocoa farm. Mahama notes that Ezra became a bully. I see that as an attempt by Ezra to mask his feelings of inferiority, which his peers were too eager to reinforce.

Those who have experienced the Ghanaian boarding school system have likely met an Ezra-like figure, someone from a remote area who gets the opportunity to study in an elite school and mix with peers from higher social classes. The intent of placing a brilliant student from the village into an elite city school is laudable. However, without deliberate efforts to help them integrate, such students may face significant prejudices and psychological pressures. It's not enough for them to excel academically; we should care about their mental well-being and protect them from class prejudice.

The need to belong

Ezra struggled partly because he didn't feel he belonged. We're social beings with an intrinsic desire to belong, to fit in. Appearing different can be uncomfortable. I learned this earlier in life. One Christmas, there was a big event that I wanted to attend. When my grandma told me to bathe before I could wear my Christmas dress, I looked her straight in the eye and said, "No way." She was firm: no bath, no Christmas dress. Stubborn me thought, "Fine, I'll just go in any shirt."

So off I went, but when I saw all the other kids dressed in fancy Christmas outfits, I felt like the odd one out. I couldn't stand it. I returned home, embarrassed to be the only one in scruffy clothes. I lied to my grandma and said I got kicked out of the event. Even as a kid, I realised how uncomfortable it was to stand out like that. I wanted to look like every other child. It shows our deep-seated need to belong; we're drawn to the warmth of human connection, the comfort of company, and the joy of shared experiences.

The Akans illustrate this with a proverb: Duikers feed in pairs as a *watchman strategy*; one keeps watch while the other eats. Duikers graze in herds not for better foliage but for the safety that numbers offer. Our foraging ancestors who adopted such herd mentality were likely to survive, reproduce, and pass down their genes.

Abraham Maslow's hierarchy of needs includes the basic need to belong. This need extends into the workplace or school, where we spend much of our lives these days. We yearn to feel that we're in the right place, around mates and colleagues with whom we can share our fears and concerns. Ezra lacked that at Achimota. I sometimes feel like Ezra.

In Munich, colleagues and neighbours differ markedly from me in many respects. This often leads to a sense of loneliness. Take the simple act of going out for lunch with colleagues, intended for bonding. It's during such dates that informal talks take place. However, I was raised to believe that talking while eating is rude. Thus, these lunch dates stress me. I'm left to choose between talking without taking a bite or eating in silence.

As a teetotaller and a non-smoker, it further complicates my social interactions. In social gatherings, abstaining from beer or coffee can subtly set you apart. I recall one off-site event in the Bavarian Alps. Some colleagues stayed out until 4 a.m., chatting. I left at 9 p.m. (the night prior), feeling out of place as the only sober person. In such gatherings, beer, coffee and cigarettes are the social lubricants. If you don't do any of them, it can leave you feeling lonely. But does this matter? The simple answer is yes.

The coronavirus pandemic forced many of us to work from home. Dahik and colleagues took the opportunity to study the impact of remote working on productivity. They surveyed 12,000 employees from the US, Germany, and India. They found that employees who felt socially connected to their colleagues (despite working remotely) kept or improved their productivity, while those who felt detached saw their performance decline. This hints at the adverse effect of feeling isolated at work.

Such lonely feelings go beyond being in a foreign country. To a lesser extent, I had similar feelings when working in Ghana. In fact, when I reflect on my move to Germany, I suspect it wasn't solely for better prospects. It's likely an unconscious attempt to escape the psychological stress of bridging the gap between my rural, blue-collar origins and corporate life in Accra. However, moving to Germany only worsened it.

I've thought of moving to an English-speaking country, hoping that the absence of a language barrier and the presence of more fellow immigrants might help. But I'm not entirely convinced this will solve the core issue of cultural dissonance. The fundamental challenges would likely persist in Canada, the UK, or the US. Besides, I once attended an event where I felt I needed a translation when a colleague from Australia spoke!

Even if I were to return to the cottage in Ghana, I doubt I would find the belongingness I once knew. The land and the people have changed. So have I. The person I was, the place I loved, and the people I knew are now shadows of their former selves.

For example, when I visit the village, some old friends relate to me strangely. At my father's funeral, I moved around, collecting chairs (for the funeral). Someone whose face seemed vaguely familiar joined me. We only had brief exchanges. It was only the next day, when I inquired about a cousin (a person with whom I had once shared a classroom), that I realised that he had been my mate in collecting the chairs. To his mind, I acted indifferently, yet I had genuinely failed to recognise him. Why didn't he talk to me?

The cultural rift between my rural life and my professional and academic world keeps widening. Conversations with my mother revolve around crop yields, while abstract theories and tools for risk analysis fill my days. If material scarcity marked my childhood in Ghana, then relational poverty shadows my current life.

The invisible bonds of kinship

The Bible relates the tale of Jephthah, who became the leader of Gilead and later fought the Ephraimites. In a cunning strategy, Jephthah's army set up checkpoints at river crossings to thwart the Ephraimites' escape. Lacking visual cues to identify them, they devised a test: suspects were asked to say *shibboleth*. The Ephraimites, unable to utter the *sh* sound, would say *sibboleth*, thus exposing their identity. This story birthed the concept of a shibboleth, which distinguishes insiders from outsiders.

Shibboleths go beyond language; they include cultural signifiers. For instance, friends from the same town and generation may share collective memories of songs and television shows, creating a bond. If you, like me, once sold kerosene in bottles at night, we might share a laugh over the quirks of that experience. Without that shared history, the humour might elude you.

I see this lack of shared experiences among footballers who, from nowhere, jumped into the limelight. I read an interview Alphonso Davies gave to the BBC, and it hinted at his struggles as a JJC. The Canadian footballer was born to Liberian parents in a Ghanaian refugee camp. At five, his family relocated to Canada. Fourteen years later, he reached the heights of professional football with Bayern Munich, winning the UEFA Champions League. In the interview, Davies said he was in awe when he entered Bayern's locker room and saw Arjen Robben.

For sure, many newcomers often feel starstruck, but Davies's class origins deepened his experience. Wayne Rooney, the former English striker, was a bit blunter. He told the *Mail on Sunday* of his struggles with sudden fame and turned to alcohol. The elephant in the room? He's from a low-income home and, thus, a JJC.

The Ghanaian music sensation Black Sherif shares a similar tale in his popular track *Soja*. A few years ago, he said, he would have dismissed any suggestion of becoming a global superstar. Now famous, he sings of his inner chaos: his anxiety, his feelings of inferiority, his heart beating fast. Another musician, Neil Young, shares a similar story. In his 1973 track *Don't Be Denied*, he talks about his childhood hardships. Despite his later success, Young confesses:

Well, all that glitters isn't gold
I know you have heard that story told
And I'm a pauper in a naked disguise
A millionaire through a businessman's eyes.

To psychologist James Grubman, JJCs are *strangers in paradise*. In this new land, they meet natives from middle-class and wealthy homes with inherent privileges. For those born into poverty or blue-collar homes, the allure of wealth is potent, yet moving to this affluent world poses a dilemma: remain true to your origins or assimilate into the new culture, its language, behaviours, and dress.

Living in this paradise of wealth, you straddle two worlds – the familiar past and the aspirational present – yet often feel like an outsider in both. The culture of paradise lacks the warmth of familiarity, while the old home feels distant and unreachable. The persistent ache of not belonging gnaws at your core.

Wearing Achilles' armour

The feeling of not belonging can lure you to masquerade as someone you are not. *Passing* is the term sociologists use to refer to such an act. Class passing is where you *pretend* to be of a higher (or lower) social class for acceptance. Since social class is often not as visible as race, engaging in class passing may be easier than racial or gender passing. But passing might weaken you. Let's return to ancient Greece to illustrate this point.

During the Trojan War, Achilles refused to continue fighting, and his friend Patroclus wore his armour and died at the hands of Hector. Hector then took Achilles' armour. When Achilles learned of Patroclus' death, he swore to avenge his friend. Achilles got a new armour and met Hector in a one-on-one battle.

Curiously, Hector was wearing Achilles' old armour, which he stripped from Patroclus. Hector's dressing gave Achilles an advantage, as he knew the armour Hector wore well. By targeting the interstice, the specific weak point where the leather didn't overlap the bronze, Achilles killed Hector with a precisely aimed spear thrust. Hector's decision to wear Achilles' armour made him weak. That's the lesson from posing as someone.

Antaeus, another figure from Greek mythology, seemed invincible. The quality stemmed from his intimate connection with the Earth, his mother. It was only when Heracles figured out the secret of Antaeus' power that he managed to overcome him, lifting Antaeus from the ground and thereby severing his source of strength. We're all like Antaeus. We derive our strength and sense of identity from our roots, the foundational experiences, relationships, and values that ground us. When you disconnect from these elements, you make yourself vulnerable.

Beyond that, there are other hidden costs of passing. A sense of identity is crucial. Passing could fuel the feeling of being a fraud (*impostor syndrome*, more later). If you're a sheep but pretend to be a goat for acceptance, you're living a lie and betraying your true self. A sheep in a goat's clothing is fake.

Passing comes with financial costs as you try to keep up with the Joneses. If you pretend to be from a wealthy home, your appearance must reflect this image. You may even change your accent to match your assumed social status. Passing in one aspect also leads to the need to pass in other areas, an idea that the philosopher Denis Diderot discussed in the eighteenth century.

Diderot received a lovely and costly scarlet dressing gown as a gift. He adored it so much that he promptly discarded his old attire. However, Diderot soon realised that his modest living space didn't match the elegance of the gown. To rectify this, he borrowed money to give his apartment new chairs, a desk, a study, a tapestry, and a bookshelf. While his room looked stylish, he sank into debt and wrote, "Poverty has its freedoms; opulence has its obstacles." By discarding his scarlet, Diderot wore Achilles' armour and became vulnerable.

Diderot's story has given us the *Diderot effect*, which describes the tendency for one purchase to trigger a chain reaction of wanting more things. Imagine buying a new phone. The new phone might make your old wristwatch look bad, so you buy a new one. Then, you see a cool new shoe that goes better with the phone and watch. It all snowballs, leading to more purchases than you initially intended. In short, buying something new can make you feel like you need more new things to go with it. We can say the same about passing; you must keep changing until you lose your identity.

If you face discrimination in more than one area, passing in one doesn't alleviate the discrimination in the other areas. For instance, if a Black woman passes as White to be accepted or enjoy certain benefits, she might still face discrimination as a woman. Consider the added challenges if she is a JJC. Passing may address one form of prejudice but doesn't ease the hurdles in other areas.

When others stigmatise you for who you are or where you come from, it may help you to resist and protest to combat the prejudice. That is because passing doesn't solve the underlying problem; it reinforces stereotypes against people like you. Also, if you pass, you indirectly pressure others in the same situation to pass, too.

I should clarify that passing differs from *code-switching*. With passing, you conceal part of yourself. On the other hand, code-switching is where you adapt to fit in while maintaining your original identity.

3: Uninvited guest at the feast

I was on my way to Pakistan in April 2018. During a layover, I visited the business class lounge at Atatürk Airport in Istanbul. Luxury surrounded me, and I felt a wave of self-doubt. Did I deserve this? Was I even qualified to talk to those high-profile people in Pakistan? This nagging doubt was no stranger; it was a constant mate.

Psychologists call this feeling *impostor syndrome.* It's that nagging voice that questions your achievements. You fear being exposed as a fraud and feel unworthy of your successes. In the late 1970s, Pauline Clance and Suzanne Imes studied this in successful women who often doubted their abilities. Later research showed it's not limited to one gender; men experience it too. Those from marginalised backgrounds usually find themselves tangled in this web of self-doubt.

As someone from a low-income, rural and illiterate background, I've felt the impact in various ways, even in Ghana. Take my rural upbringing as an example. In Ghana, people use the word *okuraseni* for those they deem uncouth, though it originally meant someone from a village. Urbanites often look down on rural folks, making mocking jokes about them.

In a way, impostor syndrome can seem rational. Humans naturally prefer the familiar; it feels safe and comforting. In ancient times, knowing your surroundings was crucial for survival, teaching our brains to favour what we know. So, while curiosity drives us to explore, new situations can stir up a deep sense of unease.

If you're someone who never imagined flying, sitting in business class can be disorienting. In a room full of people who seem so different, it's normal to question your place. The essence of impostor syndrome lies in feeling like an outsider.

Amplifying the role of luck

The idea that my success is just luck ties back to my background. When you come from a place where the odds are stacked against you, it's hard to ignore the role of external forces. There are many instances in my life where luck was crucial. So, I often feel my achievements were by grace.

If I had grown up in Munich, landing a job at Allianz or Munich Re wouldn't be surprising. However, as someone whose childhood dream was tending livestock, ending up in corporate life feels like pure luck. Most of my peers from similar backgrounds didn't go beyond elementary school, reinforcing the belief that my success is somehow luck.

Overemphasising luck can downplay hard work, but claiming full credit feels ungrateful, especially when others see my journey as grace. This perception can be psychologically coercive, making you feel guilty for downplaying external forces. Yet, overstating luck amplifies the sense of not deserving success.

The superior others

Back in Ghana, I was the go-to Excel wizard in the office. I blew everyone's minds with my ability to automate routine tasks. Fast forward to my move to Germany, and quickly, I felt like a rookie compared to my new peers. One time, I confidently offered to help a coworker with an Excel issue, only to find out his skills were way beyond mine. Talk about a reality check. I've had quite a few such ego-crash moments. I've faced challenges that made me question my abilities, leaving me unsure and feeling inadequate.

When you come from a lower social class, it's easy to view the middle and upper classes as inherently superior, seeing them as more intelligent and competent. This can make you feel intimidated in elite circles.

Imposter syndrome, under these circumstances, can seem almost rational. But it's far from pleasant. It makes you feel undeserving and fuels a relentless belief that you're a fraud. It can chip away at your confidence, fostering a secret belief that you're not as competent as others think. You always fear that your shortcomings will be exposed. It even stopped me from celebrating my successes. After defending my thesis, I didn't share the news widely, except with my younger brother. Despite sacrifices and excellent results, I felt undeserving of the title. I even worried there was an unspoken code for doctoral holders.

Similarly, when I joined Allianz in Munich, I hesitated to update my LinkedIn profile, fearing I wouldn't pass probation. Despite praise from my boss, I worried she would discover my perceived incompetence. The emotional impact was profound when she revised my performance review, saying her fondness for me might have influenced her excellent assessment. This intensified my belief I wasn't good enough. I questioned if my amiable nature got me here.

I still struggle to network, or at least in the sense of what my former boss expected. She urged me to set up lunch meetings with people I barely knew, but I often didn't, even though I knew she meant well. Given the company's size, you must become your own salesperson to be noticed. I find it hard to engage in self-promotion as it goes against everything I was brought up to believe: let your work do the talking.

Living with feelings of inferiority

I've realised that feeling inferior is normal and can be good if you handle it right. Psychotherapist Alfred Adler says these feelings can push you to improve, like a kid learning to talk by watching others. Everyone feels inferior at some point, and it's a sign of areas to work on.

Feeling inferior isn't the same as having an inferiority complex. It is when you ignore or suppress these feelings that it can block your growth. If they stick around and worsen, they might become a deep-seated complex, always hanging over you. You might then be tempted to act superior to others to feel better rather than improve yourself. This can show up as bullying, belittling, boasting, or arrogance. A superiority complex masks those insecurities.

I've learned to embrace my feelings of inferiority as a cue to improve rather than letting them turn into unhealthy complexes. Now, when I feel inferior, like when faced with a colleague's superior Excel skills, I see it as a chance to boost my skills while accepting that I can't master everything.

My struggle with impostor syndrome continues, but a mindset shift has helped. Everyone has anxieties, fears, and flaws, but many present their best selves. Or they've been raised to exude confidence, even if they're just ordinary.

Former US President Obama made this point in a recent interview with *The Pivot*. He advised, "Do not let people think you do not belong... This idea that somehow, they're so special, they're so intelligent, they're so sophisticated. Not really. They have been exposed; they have been given the confidence to feel that they belong. But if you sit down and talk to them, it turns out, mmm." He echoed the French philosopher Michel de Montaigne, who humorously noted, "Kings and philosophers shit, and so do ladies." Knowing and internalising the idea that those I see as worthy of success also have flaws and are not that special is relieving.

Besides, as an African living in Europe, you sometimes notice that people respect or admire you just for being in some circles. They might assume you come from a wealthy or privileged background or believe you must be exceptionally talented or hardworking to have made it this far. It's like your presence alone surprises them in a good way. You feel they're trying to figure out your story, wondering what makes you different or special. Sometimes, it's genuine curiosity.

Stealing a Living

In his essay and book *Bullsh*t Jobs*, the late anthropologist David Graeber discussed pointless jobs today. He argued that some jobs hinder progress toward shorter workweeks and hurt those stuck in them. While I shared Graeber's ideas, I wondered if your class origins influence how we perceive meaningful work. Moving from a blue-collar home to a white-collar job may shape perceptions.

My parents' work on the cocoa farm was physically demanding. My insurance job feels detached from that tangible reality. At first, this shift from physical work to an abstract, intellectual role made it hard for me to find fulfilment in my job. I unconsciously associated meaningful work with roles that have visible, concrete results.

In my earlier role, there were no concrete outcomes. I spent hours in meetings, organising events, and responding to emails. I struggled to feel accomplished, feeling unfulfilled and undeserving of a bonus. At the time, I would describe my job as pointless, and I didn't see the value I had added.

A chat with a senior colleague convinced me that a job's impact goes beyond immediate visibility and can manifest in unclear ways. He explained that modern organisations' connected nature means even seemingly inconsequential tasks play vital roles in overall functioning. Events I organised or attended dealing with climate change enhanced the company's reputation, attracting potential employees and customers. He helped me appreciate the subtler, indirect impact of my earlier role. Thanks a lot, Joachim!

4: Woes of the away team

One of the most talked-about streaks in English football is Chelsea's unbeaten home run in the Premier League between March 2004 and October 2008. For 1,709 days, they didn't lose a match – well, at Stamford Bridge. They played 86 home games without defeat but lost 14 times away.

So, what made them so dominant on their home turf? A big part of it was the *home advantage*. Playing football at home gives teams a psychological and practical edge, including passionate home support, familiarity with the pitch, friendlier referee decisions, less travel fatigue, and the comfort of routine.

Now, think about this in the corporate world. Some people walk into the workplace with their own version of *home advantage*. They grew up in corporate culture before they ever set foot in an office. Just like home fans can give a team an extra boost, these people benefit from built-in networks, family connections, and nurture that aligns perfectly with workplace norms. They don't have to figure out how to *act professional*; they've been absorbing it their whole lives.

The *familiarity with the pitch* in football? That's their ease in corporate spaces. They already know the unspoken rules, the office jargon, and how to handle workplace politics. Meanwhile, if you're a JJC, it can feel like stepping into a completely different world where everyone else seems to know the moves except you.

And just like a football team plays with more confidence at home, those from white-collar homes often carry themselves with a certain assurance. Not necessarily because they're better, but because they've been raised in environments that make them fit into these spaces with little or no adjustment.

For a JJC, climbing the social ladder through education is a success. Still, it doesn't automatically give you the cultural know-how to thrive in a new world. And unlike formal education, those soft skills (how to read a room, when to speak up, how to network) aren't easily learned in adulthood. They're deeply ingrained, passed down over time. No matter how you try, it's like learning a new language as an adult; you'll likely have a foreign accent.

More than just money

In his book *Habits*, the philosopher William James argued that no matter how successful you as JJC become, it's hard for you to fully adopt the style of those born into a higher social class. Here are his exact words:

Hardly ever can a youth transferred to the society of his betters unlearn the nasality and other vices of speech bred in him by the associations of his growing years. Hardly ever, indeed, no matter how much money there be in his pocket, can he even learn to dress like a gentleman-born.

In other words, your social class is more than how much money you make (*economic capital*). Who you know (*social capital*), what you know, and how you express it (*cultural capital*) also count. Winning the lottery might boost your bank balance overnight, but gaining social and cultural capital takes years of exposure and experience.

As the sociologist Pierre Bourdieu put it, your *cultural capital* includes the knowledge, skills, and refined tastes passed down through family and social circles. As the corporate *game* is played on the pitch of those from white-collar backgrounds, they tend to have an innate grasp of what's judged as *cultured* in these spaces.

Cultural capital is more about the subtle knowledge that shapes how you go about in different situations. So, if what you know is the norm, it's a huge advantage. The reverse is also true. If you grew up on a farm, you might know all about cocoa harvesting and bean processing. That expertise won't necessarily help you in the corporate world.

Malcolm Gladwell explores this idea in *Outliers*, arguing that success doesn't depend on knowledge but on *know-how*. Practical skills help people manage work and social settings.

Philosophers distinguish this as *knowledge-how* (like knowing how to ride a bike) versus *knowledge-that* (like knowing Ljubljana is the capital of Slovenia).

Much of this *know-how* comes from upbringing and surroundings. You probably learned to swim early if you grew up by the coast or had a swimming pool at home. But swimming might feel unfamiliar if you were raised in a landlocked area. The same principle applies to cultural and workplace skills. If you spent your childhood on a cocoa farm and later find yourself working in a multinational corporation, it can feel like knowing how to swim but suddenly living in the Sahara, where that skill doesn't seem to matter.

The hidden scripts of success

The point here is that as a JJC, your upbringing can put you at a disadvantage in the corporate world, especially when many of your peers grew up in environments where the skills and habits they learned as kids seamlessly translate to professional success. Take authority figures, for example. If you were raised in a home where your parents taught you to engage confidently with adults – teachers, coaches, even family friends – you're more likely to carry that confidence into the workplace. But if authority figures were mainly used to instil fear (like being threatened with "I'll call the police on you!"), you might grow up feeling intimidated by high-stakes conversations with executives.

In *Outliers*, Malcolm Gladwell highlights research showing that wealthier parents teach their kids to assert themselves, ask questions, and shape situations to their advantage. These behaviours aren't just good manners; they're a form of *cultural capital* that pays off in corporate settings, where self-assurance is key. On the other hand, children from working-class backgrounds often receive less guidance in these areas because their parents lack the time, resources, or experience to coach them.

If your parents didn't have formal education, how could they help with your homework? They might not even understand your school reports. I remember my mother once wondering aloud if weather forecasters lived in heaven. After all, how else could they predict the weather? With that level of exposure, how could she possibly provide the academic support I needed?

In the workplace, I quickly realised that many of the values I was raised with (honesty, humility, contentment) aren't necessarily assets. It took me a while to understand that being *too honest* could backfire. Once, a senior executive complimented me on a brochure design. I instinctively clarified that I hadn't designed it but had outsourced it to a professional. Later, I learned that he took this as a slight, as if I was implying I was too important to handle it personally. Should I have just smiled and said, *Thank you?* Maybe.

Over time, I learned that people don't always say what they mean in these places. What appears as a compliment could, in fact, be a critique. That speaking your mind on certain topics isn't always the best move. That there are unspoken rules you need to follow. Some of my peers had been absorbing these scripts since childhood. They know when to use charm, when to push back, when to take credit. As a JJC, you second-guess yourself.

Gladwell illustrates the power of cultural capital with two contrasting stories: Robert Oppenheimer, the brilliant physicist, and Chris Langan, a man of extraordinary intelligence who never reached his full potential. Chris, raised in a working-class home, lost his university scholarship because his mother forgot to sign a financial aid form. No one taught him how to advocate for himself. Oppenheimer, meanwhile, attempted to *poison* his professor, but instead of being expelled, he got off with a minor penalty.

Why? Because Oppenheimer knew the game. He had grown up in a wealthy home, where he learned what to say, how to say it, and who to say it to. He understood the scripts of upper-class life, while Chris, like me with the brochure, was probably just *too honest.*

Doing as the Romans do?

In the corporate world, white-collar norms set the standard, whether you like it or not. As a JJC, you may have the intelligence and qualifications, but you'll feel like an outsider without those soft skills. Your formal qualifications might help you secure the job, but it's the soft skills, which are not typically taught in school, that'll enable you to thrive.

You're pressured to fit in, even when your instincts tell you otherwise. At times, the rules directly contradict the lessons you grew up with. Take something as simple as walking. I've been told in training sessions that walking with my head up and chest out shows confidence. But where I grew up, walking with your head high wasn't just impractical; it was risky.

As a child, I walked barefoot and often stubbed my toes. My parents' advice? "Look down while walking!" It was more than avoiding painful stumbles; it was about survival. In the cottage, scorpions, snakes, and other deadly creatures lurked in the bushes. Keeping your head down was a necessity.

Imagine I grew up in Munich, where the most significant *threat* was a stray pigeon. Walking with my chest and head high would have felt natural in that world. But childhood habits, as William James tells us, stick. Although I now live in a city with no snakes to dodge, I still carry that cautious walking style. On the other hand, city dwellers strut confidently and are comfortable in their familiar, predictable environment.

A German colleague shared a story about visiting a coffee farm in Guatemala. When a fellow German saw a snake, she approached it to play with it. She had no idea it was venomous. Her urban experience had not prepared her for rural realities, just like JJCs entering the corporate world aren't often prepared for its hidden rules and risks.

Corporate jobs aren't designed with JJCs in mind. Everyone assumes you already understand the *unspoken* office norms: how to network, how to assert yourself, how to handle office politics. My job requires me to influence colleagues and business partners over whom I've no formal authority. But I was raised to respect authority figures, not to challenge or push them. A certain level of entitlement is necessary in the corporate world; it helps you to assert your needs, push for opportunities, and demand respect. Yet even something as simple as reminding a colleague to complete a task can feel uncomfortable.

For example, if I'm waiting for legal advice from a colleague who keeps delaying it, I know I should push them. A gentle nudge is often all that's needed; people are busy, after all. But I hesitate. Deep down, it still feels like I'm bothering them. I see my peers assert themselves with ease, while it takes a conscious effort for me to ask for what I deserve.

I must pick my vacation dates a year in advance. But I prefer spontaneity. I don't want to plan my relaxation twelve months ahead of time! Speaking of vacation, I still feel that getting paid while on vacation is cheating. I'm not used to it.

Familiarity breeds confidence

While writing these paragraphs and thinking of President Obama's words, *familiarity* kept popping up: being around authority figures, knowing how to wield power, and getting the hang of corporate politics and scripts. It reminded me of John MacCurdy, a famous psychiatrist and former professor at Cambridge University. He played a key role as a consultant to the British Air Force during World War II. His lectures on Air Force selection and training formed the basis of his 1943 book, *The Structure of Morale.* In it, MacCurdy explored how social class origins impact leadership aptitude.

MacCurdy didn't buy into the idea that kids from wealthy homes are naturally smarter. Instead, he argued that these kids get exposed to authority figures early on, giving them a leg up on becoming leaders. On the flip side, kids from poorer backgrounds might struggle to find the confidence needed to take charge, given their limited exposure to power structures.

MacCurdy's argument revolves around familiarity. We've all heard "familiarity breeds contempt," which means the more we know someone or something, the more likely we are to see it with disdain. For example, a physics professor might seem impressive to most people. However, to a kid who grew up around the professor, he might be a regular guy. Maybe the kid has seen the professor tipsy, heard about him failing an exam, or knows a lady who once turned him down. Knowing the professor personally, the kid realises that being a professor isn't a lofty position reserved for gods; it's something even someone with unrequited love can achieve.

In MacCurdy's view, kids from wealthier homes get familiar with power, authority, and leadership dynamics from a young age (similar to the point Obama made as we saw earlier). This familiarity gives them the confidence to handle leadership roles like they've got a backstage pass to the big show.

Recent research adds a twist to MacCurdy's ideas. A study in the US Army found that kids from higher-income households often develop a sense of entitlement. If, while growing up, they always got what they wanted without effort, they might think they deserve everything without earning it. As a Liverpool fan, I've seen a bit of that. Liverpool's past dominance makes many fans feel entitled to win every game, even when we're not the strongest team. Our history fuels that sense of entitlement.

Similarly, kids from affluent homes tend to be confident, decisive, and ambitious, traits we often link to leadership potential. But there's a catch. The same research shows a darker side: people from wealthy backgrounds can be narcissistic and have grandiose self-views. They might even bully colleagues and subordinates.

On the other hand, kids from poorer homes might have lower self-confidence. Growing up with limited resources often teaches them to cooperate and be empathetic. This upbringing leads to less entitlement and less of the typical confidence we associate with leaders. Sadly, society usually sees them as less capable, less ambitious, less committed.

To climb the ladder, you need supreme confidence and unwavering self-assurance. You must assert your opinions with conviction. Those from affluent homes will likely develop these traits, while JJCs might lean more toward humility.

So, despite your educational achievements, as a JJC, you might find it tough to reach certain managerial positions. You might lack the cultural capital that comes from growing up in affluent households and familiarity with corporate protocols and politics. JJCs might struggle with self-doubt and self-deprecating behaviour, making it hard to break the glass ceiling. That's why folks from wealthy homes often dominate leadership roles in many areas of life.

Fooled by appearances

In October 2022, the United Kingdom witnessed a significant political shift when Liz Truss resigned as Prime Minister after just 49 days. Her successor, Rishi Sunak, became one of the youngest Prime Ministers in the UK's modern history and marked a historic milestone as the country's first Prime Minister of colour. Sunak's parents, of Indian descent, had migrated from Kenya to the UK in the 1960s.

Before Sunak's rise to the premiership, another ground-breaking moment occurred with Kwasi Kwarteng's appointment as the first Black Chancellor of the Exchequer. Although his time in office was short-lived, lasting only 38 days, Kwarteng's ascension represented a significant step towards greater diversity and inclusion in the highest echelons of British politics. Or did it?

A closer look reveals an uneasy truth. Rishi and Kwasi aren't good representatives of the minority groups they come from; they come from privileged homes and boast impressive credentials. Rishi attended prestigious institutions like Winchester College, Oxford University, and Stanford University, while Kwasi's schools included Colet Court, Eton College, Cambridge University, and Harvard University.

Their privileged upbringings gave them an advantage that even most Whites don't have. The essayist Nassim Nicholas Taleb echoed this when he posted on *X* (formerly *Twitter*) on 17 July 2022: "Not a very well-known fact: the British put class way above ethnicity. Sunak…has a huge advantage over others of Anglo origin and lesser credentials."

In essence, Rishi and Boris Johnson are different sides of the same coin; their class origins hold more sway than their ethnicity. While we have made progress on racial diversity, we often sweep the equally important topic of classism under the carpet.

As inequality is a complex issue with many sides, focusing on only a few factors doesn't provide a comprehensive solution. Solving one aspect may aggravate the problem in another. A movement promoting feminism may be racist, or an anti-racism movement might be sexist. Thus, assembling a team with diverse racial and gender backgrounds isn't necessarily diversity if they all come from privileged homes (like Rishi and Kwasi).

Unfortunately, this happens even for companies genuinely committed to diversity and inclusion. You find someone from a minority group in an influential position and get excited. But after a little background check, you realise they are like Rishi.

A tangled web of biases

In disaster risk management, compound risk is when several hazards team up, creating a bigger mess than any of them would alone. Think of an earthquake that sets off a tsunami: the damage is way worse together. Similarly, when it comes to social inequalities, different types of bias can overlap, creating a web of challenges for people.

As a Black person living in Europe, my social class background, rural roots, and ethnicity all pile up to create extra hurdles in the corporate world. That's why some scholars push for intersectionality, highlighting how various social categories are connected. It emphasises the importance of widening the conversation on diversity and inclusion, recognising that people might face multiple layers of discrimination. Without considering intersectionality, efforts to tackle one type of bias, like gender bias, might miss the unique struggles of those at the crossroads of multiple marginalised identities.

On the flip side, there's a risk of sidelining certain groups, like White males from blue-collar backgrounds, when addressing racism. A White guy with a Lincolnshire accent might lack privileges and face tough challenges. Yet, he might find it hard to voice his concerns because people assume he's inherently privileged. Do these bottled-up concerns emerge in voting choices, like voting for Brexit?

My focus on social class isn't to overshadow other challenges. But discussions on diversity and inclusion often zoom in on visible aspects like ethnicity, gender, and sexuality, leaving class in the shadows. It's naive to think that once we tackle racism, Black people can compete equally. Addressing racism or sexism while ignoring classism misses the mark.

Plus, while victims of racial or gender discrimination often have support systems, those facing classism usually don't have that safety net. Countries like the UK have made racial slurs illegal, which is excellent, but class-based slurs abound. Curiously, even Microsoft Word flagged some words in this text as not inclusive, but those were racial or gender-biased words. No alerts popped up for class-biased offensive words.

Some gender activists link traits like ambition, assertiveness, confidence, decisiveness, and dominance to masculinity, while kindness, gentleness, and obedience are feminine. But it's more nuanced than that. I identify more with the so-called feminine traits. A woman from a wealthy background might show more of those *masculine* traits than I do.

Again, this isn't to downplay gender bias because even women from affluent families don't get the same breaks as their male counterparts, indicating that gender can be a barrier. But the point is, the men dominating political leadership are far from ordinary; they don't represent me.

The privileged few

Even though political leadership in Ghana might seem to rotate among various ethnic and religious groups, a closer look shows that leaders of major parties like the People's National Convention (PNC), Convention People's Party (CPP), National Democratic Congress (NDC), and the New Patriotic Party (NPP) often share privileged backgrounds, no matter their ethnicity. Take the 2012 presidential elections, for example, with candidates like Hassan Ayariga (PNC), Dr. Abu Sakara (CPP), John Mahama (NDC), and Nana Akufo-Addo (NPP).

Hassan Ayariga's dad, Frank A. Ayariga, was a Member of Parliament for the Bawku Constituency during the third republic under Dr. Hilla Limann. Dr. Abu Sakara's father, S. S. Sakara, held roles as a District Commissioner and Member of Parliament for the Damongo-Daboya Constituency during the first republic under Dr. Kwame Nkrumah. John Mahama's dad, Emmanuel A. Mahama, was a Member of Parliament for the Gonja West Constituency and a Minister of State for the Northern Region during Nkrumah's time. Nana Akufo-Addo's father, Edward Akufo-Addo, was the Chief Justice and later President of Ghana when Dr. Abrefa Busia was Prime Minister.

These folks grew up with the cultural capital for leadership roles or, as affinity bias theory suggests, saw their parents in similar positions and aspired to follow in their footsteps. Kids of political leaders are likely to soak up the rules of the political game without even trying. Plus, as I mentioned earlier, their backgrounds often arm them with traits usually tied to leadership, like self-confidence, dominance, decisiveness, and competitiveness.

5: Whistling when peeling the nuts

The tragic death of George Floyd on 25 May 2020 at the hands of police officer Derek Chauvin, who knelt on Floyd's neck for over nine minutes, sparked a global outcry against police brutality, particularly towards Black people. Floyd's desperate pleas of "I can't breathe" were ignored, leading to his sudden death. This incident made many question whether Floyd's treatment would have differed had he been White. Yet, another intriguing question arises: Would he have received a different treatment if he had worn a suit and tie?

A Zulu proverb offers a philosophical lens to view this question: *If you are peeling groundnuts for a blind man, you must keep whistling so they know you are not eating them.* This proverb suggests that when dealing with those who have reasons to doubt you, it is beneficial to signal your good character and intentions to earn their trust. We're all, in a sense, blind to each other's true motives. When meeting someone for the first time, we form opinions based on the signals they send us.

Imagine a stranger in a crowded place asking to use your mobile phone for an urgent call. Your response would likely hinge on your judgment of their character. Is the person genuinely in need, or do they intend to steal your phone? Clues such as their appearance, clothing, posture, and mannerisms help you make this judgment. While appearances can be deceiving, they are often the first thing we notice and provide initial hints about a person's intentions.

Given the limited information available, we can't help but judge books by their cover; a book's cover offers clues about its content and quality through elements like the author's name, title, font, colour, and binding. As long as we remain human, we rely on signals, and dressing can be a powerful signal of character and intention. Perhaps, if Floyd had been wearing a suit and tie (which hints at his social class), Chauvin might have given him the benefit of the doubt.

I say that out of experience. On two occasions, when I had dressed casually for flights, airline staff presumed I wasn't eligible for business class. Once, at the Air France counter in Munich, a staff member insisted I had excess luggage, surprised when I clarified I was flying business class. In another instance, someone (politely) told me I had joined the wrong queue (business class) while in line to board a Tap Portugal flight. In contrast, I've faced no such challenges when wearing a suit.

The incidents convinced me to wear a suit and tie to work, even though it's not compulsory. For those from groups burdened with negative stereotypes, signalling your credibility becomes a form of begging for the benefit of the doubt. It's like living in the same vicinity as a monster; it's wise to consider its movements when planning your travels. Thus, members of prejudiced groups may feel a psychological need to show they are exceptions, which may explain the report that Black people in the USA, on average, spend more on luxury goods. A Black person driving a Tesla signals they aren't destitute.

However, this effort to signal can be financially costly. While signalling is a natural human behaviour, over-signalling may seem necessary for a JJC to prove a point.

Little knowledge is dangerous

JJCs often feel the urge to show off their new status. It's all about fitting in or proving your place in the social pecking order. It can lead to splashing out on flashy things like fancy clothes, posh homes, and lavish parties. Take a Gucci bag, for instance; at around €900, it's a clear sign of having made it past humble beginnings. A 2010 study by Han and colleagues highlights how JJCs love these visible markers of wealth.

On the flip side, those with old money, *the patricians,* go about their lives with subtlety and grace. Their signs of class are understated, almost invisible unless you know what to look for. Think of a Bottega Veneta bag, costing a whopping €6,000, yet free from any flashy branding. The brand's logo is inside, a secret shared only among those with similar refined tastes and cultural know-how. Patricians don't feel the need to flaunt their wealth; their confidence is so deeply rooted that they don't need external validation.

The Ghanaian politician Ken Agyapong typifies this need for the new rich to flaunt their wealth. His occasional bragging about the price of his watch on national TV shows a deep psychological urge to prove he's arrived and cement his place in the social hierarchy. As someone newly wealthy, Ken Agyapong struggles with insecurities, thinking that showing off his money will earn him acceptance and respect.

But it's not just wealth that sets social classes apart; there's also the tricky thing called cultural capital, as noted earlier. Despite his considerable wealth, Agyapong finds himself lacking here. This gap was glaring during his attempt to lead his party in 2023. Colleagues and those who've benefited from his generosity questioned his presidential capabilities, pointing to his unpolished remarks as evidence of his lack of cultural refinement.

In trying to prove yourself as a JJC, you risk overdoing it. It's easy to go overboard when you're deprived of something for a long time and finally get to experience it. Carl Jung's notion of *enantiodromia* explains this. It's the idea that an extreme or repressed state will eventually flip to its opposite. So, after long-term deprivation, the pent-up desire can lead to excess once the opportunity arises.

Looking back, I wasn't fully aware at first, but I suspect choosing my locality was a way to flaunt my status. When I moved to my current area, a suburb in Munich, a neighbour was curious about my job, thinking it odd for a Black person to live there. By living here, I wanted to show that, despite my ethnicity, I defied typical labels associated with African migrants. I tried to convey that I hadn't trekked through the Sahara Desert to get here.

Though moving here might have been an unconscious decision, I deliberately use my official email address when communicating with my kids' school. In Germany, pupils are divided into different secondary schools after fourth grade. Factors like academic ability, self-confidence, independence, and family background influence these decisions. As primary school teachers recommend students for specific schools, using my official email (with my academic title) was my way of subtly indicating that, despite my shaky German, my educational credentials are solid.

It was a smart move, as both my daughters went to Gymnasium, the school for academically inclined students. I read on *Deutsche Welle* that only 27 per cent of kids whose parents didn't attend university go to Gymnasium, compared to over 80 per cent of those with university-educated parents. Showing my academic credentials might have helped shape my children's future.

Banana republic dictator

A JJC may feel the need to show off to mask their insecurities. In a sense, it mirrors the human condition. Historian Yuval Noah Harari touches on this in *Sapiens,* arguing that humans' *sudden* rise to the top of the food chain left us unsettled and anxious. We're more like a banana republic dictator desperately clinging to power.

For most of history, we weren't the kings of the jungle. We were just another species scrapping for survival, competing with scavengers for leftovers. But then, we made tools, learned to control fire, and (almost overnight) became the planet's dominant force. Unlike lions, sharks, or eagles, which evolved into apex predators over millions of years, we shot to the top in an evolutionary blink. The problem? We never really *grew into* the role. The world didn't have time to adjust, and neither did we.

That's why, deep down, we still struggle with insecurity. Harari suggests this insecurity makes us treat other creatures wickedly. There's some truth in that. As Seneca noted, "All cruelty springs from weakness."

Flying too close to the sun

Feeling inadequate can push you to extremes. As a JJC, you might be bouncing between being too aggressive or timid, too ambitious or too hesitant. It's like you're either trying too hard to prove yourself or holding back too much out of fear.

A great metaphor for this comes from Greek mythology. When Daedalus and his son Icarus were trapped in a tower by King Minos, Daedalus crafted wings out of feathers and wax to escape. Before taking off, he warned Icarus: "Don't fly too high, or the sun will melt the wax. But don't fly too low either, or the sea's moisture will weigh you down."

But Icarus got carried away. Wanting to impress sailors watching from below, he soared higher and higher until the wax melted, his feathers scattered, and he plunged into the sea. Icarus's story perfectly shows how sudden success can breed overconfidence. When you achieve something beyond your expectations, it's easy to start believing you're invincible. This happens to people constantly, especially JJCs trying to prove themselves. You push too hard, overextend, and sometimes crash like Icarus.

But remember, Daedalus didn't just warn Icarus about flying too high. He also warned him about flying too low. If he flew too close to the sea, his wings would get soaked, and he wouldn't be able to rise.

JJCs often face this exact dilemma. You might feel the need to prove yourself, pushing too hard and risking burnout. Or you might shrink back, afraid to take up space, keeping yourself from growing. Neither extreme helps in the long run. The key is to find balance. Aim high, but not so high that you lose control. Stay grounded, but not so low that you hold yourself back.

When there is something to lose

One of the hidden traps a JJC can fall into is risk aversion, precisely because they now have something to lose. Consider the following football analogy. The 2019 UEFA Champions League final saw Liverpool face Tottenham Hotspur in Madrid. Liverpool had narrowly missed out on the Premier League title to Manchester City, and another defeat would have cast a shadow over an otherwise spectacular season.

Liverpool won the final, but the match statistics painted a different picture. Tottenham dominated possession with 65 per cent, completing 510 passes compared to Liverpool's 272. This starkly contrasted with Liverpool's usual style, where they averaged 606 passes per game in the Premier League that season. Why did they play so cautiously?

Their early goal in the second minute made them risk-averse; they had something to protect. Meanwhile, Tottenham, with nothing to lose, attacked relentlessly. Whether they lost 1-0 or 5-0 made little difference; their only chance was to take risks.

Nobel laureate Daniel Kahneman's *Thinking, Fast and Slow* explains how our perception of risk shifts depends on whether we are in a position of potential gain or loss.

Imagine you have a 95 per cent chance of winning $10,000. That slight 5 per cent uncertainly gnaws at you, making the possibility of *not* winning feel highly significant. If someone offers you $9,000 upfront to walk away from the gamble, you might take it, preferring certainty over the small risk of losing everything.

Now, flip the scenario. Suppose you have a 95 per cent chance of *losing* $10,000. That slim 5 per cent chance of escaping loss suddenly feels huge. If someone offers to let you pay $9,000 to avoid the full $10,000 loss, you're likely to reject it. The mere possibility of dodging the loss entirely makes you cling to risk.

This explains why Tottenham played boldly in the 2019 final while Liverpool played it safe. When you've little to lose, risks seem more attractive. But when you stand on the edge of success, the fear of losing what you've built can paralyse you.

We saw a similar pattern during the COVID-19 lockdowns in Ghana. People living in poverty were more likely to defy restrictions. Staying home meant *certain* hunger. Venturing outside carried some risk of catching the virus, but it also held the *possibility* of survival. With no good options, they took the risk. Meanwhile, those with food security saw things differently and followed the rules.

The same logic drives African youth to risk their lives crossing the Sahara Desert in pursuit of Europe. When the future at home feels hopeless, even a risky journey seems worth trying. But those with better prospects hesitate to gamble what they already have.

Paradoxically, the *old rich* can afford to take risks because their wealth is diversified. A failed venture is just a setback, not a tragedy. For a JJC, however, the stakes feel much higher. Without a financial cushion or a generational safety net, even a *small* risk of failure can loom large. There are things I could do independently, yet the possibility of failure makes me hesitate. Ironically, the courage that once propelled me forward now feels dampened by caution.

This is the paradox of the JJC: You may become so afraid of losing what you have that you stop taking the risks that once defined you. Conversely, you may let modest success inflate your confidence, leading you to reckless, ruinous decisions. Either extreme is dangerous. Recognising this dilemma is the first step toward striking the right balance between caution and ambition.

Beyond reproach

One of the biggest challenges for a JJC is the lack of people willing or able to offer honest, constructive criticism. As you climb the social ladder, those who might have corrected you before may now hesitate. They either lack the confidence to call you out or worry about jeopardising their relationship with you.

But no matter who you are, having someone to call you out on your mistakes is priceless. We often take this for granted, but constructive criticism serves as a mirror, revealing blind spots we might otherwise ignore. It provides an external perspective, helping us grow, refine our skills, and avoid complacency. Without it, there's a risk of becoming disconnected from reality.

Criticism, when given in the right spirit, fosters resilience and self-awareness. It keeps you grounded, helps you course-correct, and makes you stronger. I sometimes crave honest feedback, someone who can tell me, "You're going too far."

6: New wine in old wineskins

In 2013, a researcher from Charité–Universitätsmedizin Berlin invited me to participate in a study that examined the rates of obesity and type-2 diabetes among Ghanaians living in Berlin. The study compared the lifestyles of Ghanaians in rural and urban Ghana against those in Berlin, Amsterdam, and London. Blood samples were collected, and I was asked to complete an exhaustive questionnaire detailing my dietary habits.

By 2016, the study's findings were published, painting a rather sombre picture. In rural Ghana, the prevalence of obesity was about one per cent among men and eight per cent among women. The figures escalated in urban Ghana, with seven per cent of men and an alarming 40 per cent of women being classified as obese. The situation was even more dire for Ghanaians in Europe, particularly in London, where one in five Ghanaian men and a shocking half of Ghanaian women were obese.

The study similarly highlighted the prevalence of type-2 diabetes. In rural Ghana, 4 per cent of men and six per cent of women were diabetic. In urban areas, these rates surged to 10 per cent for men and 9 per cent for women. Among Ghanaians living in Berlin, 15 per cent of men and 10 per cent of women were diabetic. These findings contribute to the growing body of evidence that Ghanaian migrants in Europe are more susceptible to type 2 diabetes and obesity compared to both the local European populations and Ghanaians living in Ghana. Migrants from other sub-Saharan African countries face similar challenges.

The research didn't explain the reasons behind these alarming statistics; future studies may shed light on the contributing factors and guide appropriate interventions. Meanwhile, we can make educated guesses about the stark differences between Ghanaian migrants and Europeans. Do Ghanaians in Europe consume different foods compared to their European counterparts? If Ghanaians in Europe still adhere to their traditional diet, what accounts for the vast disparities between them and Ghanaians in Ghana?

Less physical activities

One plausible, even if prosaic, explanation could be the difference in physical activity levels between Ghanaians and Europeans. In many rural parts of Ghana, where transportation is a significant challenge, people often walk long distances to carry out their daily routines. Many also perform manual labour, particularly in farming. Conversely, those living in urban areas have easy access to transportation and have sedentary jobs, seldom using stairs and preferring lifts. Thus, they engage in fewer physical activities.

In Germany, I frequently observe Whites participating in activities such as jogging, cycling, and other forms of exercise. I rarely see Africans doing that consistently. Thus, the differences in physical activity levels could explain why Ghanaians living in Europe are more susceptible to obesity and diabetes than Europeans.

Joining old and new garments

Another factor worth considering is our childhood diet. Clinical epidemiologist David Barker argues that our early upbringing can have a lasting impact on our health. According to Barker, the body adapts to insufficient nutrients if you experience malnutrition during infancy or before birth. This adaptation leads to permanent changes in the body's physiology and metabolism. In other words, if your body requires 500 calories to function optimally but only receives 300 calories, it adjusts to this reality and undergoes permanent changes.

Thus, when you've experienced malnutrition and later escape poverty as an adult, the body may be primed for only 300 calories. If you consume 500 calories, the body may react poorly to the "excess" of 200 calories. These excess calories make you susceptible to obesity, diabetes, insulin insensitivity, and high blood pressure. Barker's idea is now known as the Baker hypothesis.

Baker's idea has some legs to stand on. An earlier study that followed the lives of 16,000 people born in

Hertfordshire, UK, found a link between low birth weight (indicative of limited nutrient intake) and the later development of coronary heart disease. Subsequent studies in the USA and India have also confirmed this link between low birth weight and coronary heart disease.

I liken the Baker hypothesis to combining an old garment with a new one or, to be Biblical, pouring new wine into old wineskins. When a new cloth has not yet shrunk, using it to patch an older garment would cause a tear as it begins to shrink. Similarly, an old wineskin becomes brittle after holding fermented wine and reusing it, which could cause it to burst.

The Baker hypothesis may partly explain why those born and raised in Ghana may be more susceptible to obesity and type 2 diabetes when they gain access to high-energy foods in urban areas or Europe. Many pregnant women in Ghana, especially in rural areas, don't receive sufficient essential nutrients during their pregnancies to meet their nutritional requirements. While this may not pose a significant challenge if the children continue to live in rural areas and consume low-energy diets, challenges related to metabolic syndrome arise when they move to urban areas in Ghana or Europe and begin to eat high-energy diets.

Traditional Ghanaian cuisine consists of starchy foods like yam, cocoyam, cassava, plantain, corn, or rice. These were the staple foods I consumed daily during my upbringing. The main dish was *fufu*, made from cassava and yams (or plantains). Fufu is typically rich in carbohydrates but lacks sufficient nutrients. If your body has adapted to such foods and you switch to more nutritious meals, the Baker hypothesis suggests it might be unhelpful.

Meat for adults

Moreover, growing up in Ghana, many children did not eat much meat because it was expensive or because adults got the best pieces. So, when you grow up, meat may be seen as a status symbol. You may overcome meat to compensate for what was missed. This habit can lead to health problems, especially when combined with other unhealthy habits.

Since I live in Europe, it can be tempting to indulge in city meals. While these foods may offer a more balanced diet, my body, accustomed to village starchy cuisine, may respond differently. So, I make a conscious effort to limit them. Some friends back in Ghana often remark that I have not changed much since moving to Germany (they expect me to gain weight now that I live in Europe). I am cautious about what I eat, even if my colleagues, who have been eating these foods from infancy, consider them healthy.

There is ample scientific evidence that our social class origins influence our health. For instance, a 2010 study revealed that those with lower-income parents experience poorer health and higher mortality rates. This issue extends to JJCs, as they face the dual challenge of adapting to diets unknown to their bodies.

While we await further research and the need for a thorough understanding of these matters to develop effective preventive strategies, I opt to consume my village's less nutritious food. It can be costly in Europe, but switching diets might be more expensive. Poverty, it seems, lingers even after one escapes its grips.

7: Which one should the two become?

While living on Mount Ida, Paris married the nymph Oenone. Their life together was simple and down-to-earth, which reflected their shared background. But everything changed when Paris left behind his rural life and stepped into the grandeur of the Trojan Palace.

Then came Helen: stunning, legendary, practically divine. Paris was captivated, drawn into a world of luxury and sophistication that couldn't have been more different from what he had with Oenone. His attraction to Helen showed how his desires and ambitions were shifting.

Paris' story with Helen is a classic case of love crossing social boundaries, bringing all the complications that come with such relationships. It's the struggle between sticking with what's familiar and chasing something new and exciting. Should people seek partners from similar backgrounds, or does love transcend all that?

Dumping your class

In her book *Get to Work*, activist Linda Hirshman presents a provocative thesis that challenges conventional wisdom about women's roles in society. She argues that women should prioritise their careers rather than sacrificing their professional ambitions on the altar of marriage or family. Hirshman encourages women to pursue deeply fulfilling work and not let traditional domestic roles hinder their career growth.

One of the more intriguing aspects of her argument is that women might benefit from marrying *down* (financially or socially less advantaged men). Her logic is that such a dynamic could give women a stronger bargaining position within the union. For instance, a less physically attractive man might have fewer potential partners, which could make him more loyal and committed. After all, he might feel less confident in finding other attractive partners. In contrast, a more handsome man might have a wider array of options, potentially making him less devoted.

Hirshman's views sparked extensive debate, as they contradict the prevailing norms. While love may transcend boundaries, we tend to choose partners similar to us, known as *homophily* or *assortative mating*. We are more likely to form and sustain romantic relationships with people who share our physical attractiveness, social status, values, intelligence, and other traits. This similarity fosters a sense of security and mutual respect within the relationship.

However, we sometimes choose partners who differ from us (*heterophily*). For example, you might prefer a partner from a different social class than yours. Heterophily could involve marrying up (*hypergamy*) or marrying down (*hypogamy*). Such choices can offer their unique forms of enrichment and challenge.

Historically, men and women have approached the institution of marriage with differing strategies. Men have tended to *marry down,* while women have sought to *marry up.* This pattern is deeply rooted in patriarchal norms that have traditionally positioned men as the primary breadwinners, thereby opposing unions where men might marry above their social station.

Conversely, women have often married up to secure their future, a practice reinforced by societal expectations, cultural practices, and even legal frameworks. In ancient Rome, for instance, laws dictated marital choices based on social status, encouraging women to marry men of equal or higher standing and discouraging unions with those beneath them.

The notion of women marrying up remains pervasive in many societies. Women are frequently judged by their partner's social and economic status and face societal pressure to marry into higher social classes or, at the very least, to remain within their own. Linda Hirshman argues that this expectation can harm a woman's career advancement, positing that marrying down might afford women more influence and autonomy.

When you reflect on Hirshman's idea, it becomes evident that the nuances of marrying up or down hinge on whether we reference your current class or your class origins. This distinction is crucial. Two people may share the same white-collar class status but hail from different origins. If a JJC (someone with blue-collar roots but now has a white-collar job) marries someone who shares those origins but not their current class, is this marrying down? Then again, is this assortative mating if a JJC marries someone who shares their current class but not their origins?

For a JJC, finding another JJC as a partner can be challenging. Yet, marrying someone who shares your blue-collar origins but has not undergone the same class migration might not be appealing, as it could remind you of the distance you have travelled. This creates a tension between the desire for connection and the risk of regression. Your worldview diverges from those who share your background but have not experienced the same journey.

Does this suggest a JJC should marry someone who shares their current white-collar status even if they come from a different class origin? There are compelling arguments for this. Opposites attract. The differences in class origins can be intriguing and exciting initially. As a JJC, your partner's different lifestyle, perspectives, or experiences might be attractive. For instance, the partner from a white-collar origin might find the grounded, practical perspective from the JJC appealing. Conversely, the JJC might admire their patrician partner's confidence.

However, a JJC marrying someone who shares their current class but comes from a different origin is also fraught with challenges. We carry the cultural capital of our upbringing into new social contexts. Our class origins shape our lifestyles, expectations, and values. Paris and Helen had different lifestyles. Could Paris balance Helen's luxurious life and expensive hobbies with his simpler lifestyle? As a JJC, you may be unable to socialise comfortably with your patrician partner's friends and family. Even if your partner understands and excuses your lack of class, their family might not.

Your quest for a meaningful romantic relationship places you at a crossroads. Returning to your roots to find someone who shares your origins can be a double-edged sword. While shared experiences may foster a sense of comfort, your partner may remain steeped in the struggles you have fought to overcome. Yet, choosing someone who shares your current class but comes from a different origin means you might find their lifestyle alien. Given the rarity of fellow JJCs, you may end up with someone who does not share your background. Let us look at some of the challenges that the JJC might face.

The power of the past

Sociologist Jessi Streib explores the world of inter-class marriages, focusing on highly educated folks who marry partners from different social class backgrounds. She looks at the dynamic between *parvenus* (those moving from blue- to white-collar) and *patricians* (those staying within the white-collar realm). Through interviews with these couples, Streib found that even though both partners now live in the white-collar social class, their origins leave a lasting mark, sometimes subtle, sometimes obvious. She argues that your class origins significantly impact married life more than your current class status, shaping how you instinctively react to everyday situations.

People from white-collar backgrounds often take what Streib calls a "managerial approach" to life. They plan their spending, career paths, leisure activities, and even manage their emotions with care. On the flip side, JJCs tend to have a more laid-back attitude, marked by impulsive spending, unstructured leisure time for themselves and their kids, and a freer expression of emotions. This difference ties back to the earlier conversation about how high- and low-income families raise their kids differently.

Streib points out that some of her interviewees felt a stronger connection with strangers who shared their class origins than with their own partners. These couples often wrestle with different philosophies on living, using resources, and raising kids. Even though they've climbed the social ladder, a JJC's roots remain a big part of their identity, which can lead to clashes over traditions, values, and expectations. It can be tempting for patricians to try to shape their JJC partner to fit their tastes.

Unsustainable path

If you're a JJC and find yourself in a relationship where your non-JJC partner pushes you to fit into their mould instead of meeting halfway. Big mistake! If you give in too much because you feel a bit out of your depth, you might end up sidelining your own wants and needs. Even if your partner acts up, you might let it slide just to keep the peace. But letting lousy behaviour go unchecked can set a dangerous precedent, and your silence might come across as agreement.

Playing the people-pleaser game (going all out for your partner's approval or always putting their needs first) might seem sweet, but it can lead to resentment. You might end up feeling taken advantage of or undervalued, which can fill the relationship with negativity. If you only speak up when things get unbearable, it might catch your partner off guard, leaving them confused by the sudden shift. Letting issues simmer can lead to explosive reactions later, where even small things set you off.

Avoiding tough truths to keep the peace can be damaging in the long run. If a pendulum swings too far one way, it'll swing back to find balance (enantiodromia). This means ignoring or burying negative feelings can make them pop up unexpectedly. Your mind naturally seeks balance, so suppressing parts of yourself can lead to those parts demanding attention later.

The key is to set boundaries early to keep the relationship healthy and avoid unpleasant surprises. Remember, the traits that first attracted you to your partner might later annoy you. Their confidence might start feeling arrogant, and they might see your down-to-earth vibe as lacking ambition.

This isn't to say JJCs are saints and everyone else isn't. Though rare, a JJC might try to shape their partner to fit their ideals instead of communicating openly and appreciating each other's perspectives. No matter how you look at it, marrying someone who doesn't respect where you come from is a bad idea. Choose someone who takes pride in you and doesn't see being with you as doing you a favour.

Marriage should be about finding that one person out of over eight billion who will embrace your inner child, stand by you, lift your spirits, celebrate your wins, face life's challenges with you, listen when things get tough, accept your quirks, and inspire you to grow without trying to change you. If this person can't speak kindly about you, whether to your face or behind your back, then who will?

A prophet without honour

When you start, you're probably not rolling in cash. Your partner sees the real, unfiltered version of you: the struggles, the setbacks, the grind to build a better life. They know exactly where you've come from.

But as time goes on, things change. You climb the ladder, find success, and life gets much cushier. Your partner might struggle to shake off that old image of you. Even as you grow, they still see the person who had to fight for everything. It's like that saying: "A prophet has no honour in their own land."

Now, take someone who meets you after you've made it. To them, you're just this polished, successful person, maybe even a bit of a hero. They don't know the backstory, so their admiration comes easy. Meanwhile, your partner, who's been there through thick and thin, might not give you that same starry-eyed recognition.

And let's be honest, everyone likes to feel appreciated for their wins. When your partner, stuck in the past, doesn't quite see how far you've come, it can sting, especially when others *do* see it. It's not that your partner loves you any less, but that old history can make it harder for them to celebrate the new you.

No one's to blame here, but that gap between past and present can quietly cause tension. Your partner's love is solid, but if the praise you crave comes more from outsiders than them? That can hurt. It's a clash of memories and milestones; the heart's still in it, but the mind takes longer to catch up.

Climbing Mount Maslow

Let us now focus on the primary reason for getting married, which might be a source of tension when a JJC is involved. Marriage, at its core, is a complex institution. To understand its motivations, we might turn to Abraham Maslow's hierarchy of needs, which suggests that our desires are layered like a pyramid. We find our basic needs: food, water, and shelter.

Above these are our safety needs, encompassing a sense of security in our minds, bodies, and finances. Next, we encounter the need for love and belonging –having friends, being close to someone, trusting, and feeling emotionally connected. At the top, we find the higher-level needs, which involve feeling good about ourselves, growing as individuals, and reaching our full potential.

Psychologist Eli Finkel and colleagues have examined American marriages through historical and psychological lenses. They argue that the primary reasons for marriage in America have evolved. They use the concept of Mount Maslow to illustrate that contemporary Americans have different expectations of marriage compared to the past. In the mid-1800s and earlier, marriage was often about meeting basic needs like food, shelter, protection, and financial security. Given the harsh economic realities of the time, love was often a luxury, and parents frequently played a significant role in choosing your spouse.

As America became more economically prosperous and urbanised from the 1850s onwards, the focus of marriage shifted to love. Technological advancements made it easier for people to meet their basic needs, leading them to seek companionship, emotional connection, and love within marriage. This Romantic era persisted until the 1960s. During this period, people could find love and even sexual satisfaction outside of marriage, influenced by the availability of pornography and a more liberal attitude towards premarital sex.

It is crucial to note that romantic love has always been celebrated in literature and art, even when marriages were primarily about meeting basic needs. Couples often experienced strong emotional connections, but love was not always the primary reason for marriage.

Today, marriage is not solely about love. People may marry for various reasons, including fulfilling higher-level needs such as self-esteem and personal growth. The American study indicates that while safety and love remain important, people expect more from their marriages. This trend is not limited to the US; as many parts of the world advance economically, people's motivations for marriage evolve similarly.

Even in developing countries, where many still struggle to meet basic needs, not everyone is solely focused on survival. Some people may marry in these places to achieve self-fulfilment and personal growth, while others prioritise basic needs. For example, the middle class in Accra often leads lifestyles akin to those in London despite financial constraints.

In Ghanaian towns and villages, where most people are peasant farmers, marriage still serves to meet basic needs like food, clothing, and shelter. However, Western cultural influences are evident in urban areas and among Ghana's middle class. These people often experience nuclear family structures, white-collar work, regular outings, family vacations abroad, and financial independence.

From the American study, we can infer that white-collar people in developing countries marry to fulfil higher-level needs. They value the "little things" their partners do for them, seeking companionship, affection, and thoughtful gestures. They appreciate acts like going out together, remembering special occasions, and displays of chivalry.

When a JJC and a patrician enter a romantic relationship, their differing family backgrounds shape their views on marriage. A JJC might see marriage as a way to meet basic needs like food, shelter, water, and sexual intimacy. They might feel they are doing well if they provide these necessities. However, their partner from a wealthy background might view marriage as a means to satisfy other needs, such as love and emotional connection. Their attitudes towards money may also differ, with the JJC perceiving their partner as extravagant for spending on non-essential items.

If you are a JJC, understanding the diverse motivations and expectations that others bring to relationships can be beneficial. Of course, motivations for marriage can change over time, influenced by cultural shifts, economic progress, and individual aspirations.

A blind leading the blind

This chapter is a perfect spot to discuss the challenges JJCs face when raising kids. So, how do you raise kids to thrive in a world of affluence when your own roots are grounded in more humble beginnings? Do you teach them the language of your origins, rich with the rhythm of your history and struggles, or do you switch to the vernacular of your new class, full of ease and luxury?

You're in limbo as a parent who's climbed the social ladder. You remember the lessons from scarcity, the resilience, resourcefulness, and joy in small things. Yet now you're living in a world where abundance is the norm, and you naturally want to share this comfort with your kids. The trick is managing this balance without losing the essence of either world.

You might want to give your kids what you missed: a sense of security and the freedom to chase their passions without worrying about money. But there's always the fear of raising kids who might crumble at the first sign of trouble. You don't want to create a gilded cage where every need is met, leaving no room for them to develop grit and independence.

In this balancing act, you're trying to instil in your kids the values that shaped you (hard work, empathy, and gratitude) while letting them enjoy the fruits of your labour. You share the language of your origins, not as a relic but as a living testament to your journey. You teach them the language of your present so they can thrive in their current world.

The goal is to raise kids comfortable in their privileged surroundings and connected to the broader human experience. You want them to have humility and awareness, recognising that their current reality is just one of many possible lives. You hope to bridge the gap between your past and future worlds, creating a harmonious blend that honours both. And that, my friend, is no small feat!

The toilet bowl

From the foregoing, it might seem I'm against a JJC marrying someone from a higher social class background. Far from it. Awareness of these potential challenges could help to avert or manage them. I like to think of it as the toilet bowl.

Have you ever wondered where most germs lurk in your home? If you guessed the toilet bowl, think again. It turns out that the real offenders are things like dish sponges and cutting boards. It makes sense if you think about it. We tend to be cautious based on how risky we believe something is. We're diligent about disinfecting the toilet because we know it's a hotspot for bacteria. That's called *risk compensation*; we adjust our behaviour to manage the risks we know.

Now, this idea has a lot to do with relationships. If you're aware of the potential challenges beforehand, you know you'll have to work on your relationship if you want it to succeed. You understand the *risk* of building a life with someone different. It opens doors to communication, compromise, and growth.

The truth is, living with someone else, someone who's different from you and flawed (just like you are), is never going to be smooth sailing. Loving someone takes constant effort to keep things healthy. We must treat relationships like the toilet bowl: something that requires attention and care, irrespective of the class backgrounds of those involved.

8: Helping mum to lose her teeth

As I grew up on a cocoa farm, allow me to share some practices. Cocoa farming in Ghana is more than just agriculture; it stands for teamwork. Due to its labour-intensive nature, the process requires many hands to plant and dry beans. Relying on collective effort isn't just practical but serves as a social contract among farmers.

When farmers gather to break pods, the occasion goes beyond work. When the farmers meet to support fellow farmers, they share stories, discuss the highs and lows of their work, and find solace in their shared experiences. To make it even more fun, the host can hide a can of corned beef among the cocoa pods, and the finder keeps it as a prize.

An unspoken rule governs this mutual aid system: contributing to the group is essential to benefit from it. A farmer who prioritises personal gain over community risks exclusion. In truth, this principle reflects Ghanaian culture, where the collective needs trump individual desires. Indeed, Ghana scores a mere nine per cent on a scale that measures individualism. In stark contrast, Germany scores 79 per cent. This means that Germans emphasise "I" and "me" more, while Ghana prioritises "we" and "us."

While this collectivist spirit is helpful in many ways, it can pose challenges for JJCs. As one of the few success stories in the family, the JJC faces intense pressure to meet extended family expectations. This is known as the black tax among the Africans in the diaspora. It describes the financial obligations that successful Africans feel towards their extended families, including support for bills, education, and other expenses.

Former Nigerian and Chelsea footballer Mikel Obi recently highlighted the burden of the black tax. In an interview, he stated the silent pressure on successful Africans: "When you come from Africa... when you make money, it's not your money... All you do is keep giving; they're so comfortable that they expect you to do that for the rest of your life."

A single tree against the winds

As the Akans say, *When a single tree faces the gale, it snaps.* This proverb illustrates the vulnerability of being the sole or one of the few successful people in your family. If only a few trees in a forest grow tall, they're more susceptible to being toppled by strong winds. Similarly, if you're the only one or one of the few to escape poverty, the pressure from your family's expectations can feel like a storm threatening to undo your achievements.

In a sense, those demands are valid. I'm indebted to this tradition. From childhood, my extended family has always supported me, caring for me while my parents worked on their cocoa farm. So, now that I am financially stable, there's an unspoken expectation to give back, a moral and cultural duty. The dictum goes: *If someone has cared for you while growing your teeth, you should also care for them when they lose theirs.*

The fact that I live abroad increases people's expectations of me. Many believe that once you live abroad, there's nothing you cannot do. The wicked uncle abroad is a familiar figure in Ghana, the relative who fails to meet endless financial requests from home. While declining requests for luxury items like the latest iPhone is easy, saying no to essential needs like medical bills or school fees is much harder. Not fulfilling these demands can lead to guilt, especially when spending on oneself.

In May 2019, I travelled to Geneva for a conference. The city's serenity, particularly the strolls along Lake Geneva, charmed me. It evoked positive emotions and made me feel at ease. A few days later, I went to Ghana for work and took the opportunity to reconnect with my father's cocoa farm and old friends. Despite my best efforts to help, I realised my support was only a temporary solution. The contrast between my luxurious travels and the struggles I saw made me feel guilty.

Escaping poverty when friends remain trapped can evoke feelings of unearned privilege. How do you justify a trip to

Paris to see the Mona Lisa when that money could significantly aid someone back in Ghana? These sentiments might seem odd if you're from an individualistic culture. So, let me break it down a bit further.

Did you come empty-handed?

In Ghana, as in many African countries, loyalty to extended family is vital. There's no word for cousin; cousins are siblings, and your mum's sister is another mum, not just an aunt. If you join me to visit my family in Ghana, I would introduce four women as my mum: my biological mum and her three sisters. Extended families are so close-knit that buying life insurance might seem to betray the communal spirit. Are you finding a private solution instead of relying on collective responsibility?

You may even be expected to accept extended family members in your home. This can potentially strain the relationship with your partner. Maintaining extended family harmony while preserving peace at home is one challenge you will likely confront as a JJC.

Beyond these extended family members, you even owe the larger society some responsibility. For example, returning home involves bringing gifts for family, friends, and strangers. Ian Utley's guidebook on Ghana has a joke that illustrates this expectation. Kojo and Kofi, two friends who hadn't seen each other since school days in Ghana, reunite in New York. As they part, Kojo invites Kofi to visit his apartment. The conversation unfolds:

Kojo: I have a wife and three children and would love you to visit us.

Kofi: Great. Where do you live?

Kojo: Here is the address. And there is a parking space behind the apartment. Once parked, use your foot to give a gentle kick to the front door, go ahead to the elevator, and press the button using your left elbow. Enter the elevator and ride it up to the sixth floor. Walk down the hallway until you spot my name on the door. Use your right elbow to press the doorbell, and I'll open the door to welcome you inside.

Kofi: Good. But tell me. What is all this business of kicking the front door open and pressing the elevator with my left and right elbows?

Kojo: Surely you're not coming empty-handed?

The expectation of giving gifts is so ingrained that it may feel unsettling or even concerning if no one asks for them. Being asked for gifts acknowledges your community ties. Failing to meet these expectations can induce guilt as if you've let everyone down.

This tradition can strain your finances and emotions. I learned pretty early to set a sensible budget for helping others. Once it's drained, I politely decline further requests. It also helps to invest in long-term plans that automatically deduct from your bank account, ensuring there's no excess cash available. This approach can allow you to say no without guilt. It's much harder to refuse when money is readily accessible.

A *Kollege* is not a friend

In Germany, workplace culture is more individualistic. Despite working closely with colleagues, I haven't formed close personal relationships with most, except Joachim S. None know where I live, and their private contact information remains private. Collegial relationships can be friendly, but there's a clear boundary between professional and personal life. Germans often distinguish work from personal relationships.

I shared a close working relationship with one colleague, often having lunch together and occasionally walking in the nearby English Garden. However, I was absent on her last day, and upon returning, I found a note on my keyboard: "Lieber Benji, Auf Wiedersehen, B" *(Dear Benji, goodbye, B)*. I expected her contact details, but she didn't leave any, indicating our relationship was strictly professional.

In Ghana, such a gesture might be perceived as a personal offence. But my former colleague viewed it as a standard parting gesture. Germans maintain close bonds with childhood friends, making it challenging for newcomers to integrate and form deep connections. Despite living in Germany for over a decade, I don't have a German friend. While it might be tempting to attribute this to racism, I believe it has nothing to do with that.

A German colleague shared his experience moving from his village to Munich. He tried to introduce himself to his neighbours by knocking on their doors but saw varied reactions. Some didn't open their doors despite being home; others opened their doors but remained silent, and one was surprised by the gesture.

You may be right

Another cultural nuance involves how Germans perceive and interact with power. Social psychologists use power distance to classify cultures based on the extent to which people expect and accept unequal power dynamics. Ghana scores 80 per cent, indicating acceptance of hierarchical structures without questioning authority. In contrast, Germany scores 35 per cent, thus encouraging juniors to challenge superiors.

A biblical parable shows this difference. Jesus shares a story of a man with two sons, instructing them to work in his vineyard. The first son initially refuses but later complies, while the second agrees but does not follow through. According to the Bible, despite initially refusing, the first son finally does the right thing by going to work. In Ghanaian culture, openly defying a father's request is rude. So, the second son did the right thing. In Ghana, people often use indirect phrases like "You may be right" or "I'll think about it" to decline politely.

I recall a project we had in Ghana. My German colleague, with whom we were managing the project, was often excited when we met the stakeholders in Ghana, and they showed interest. I always cautioned him not to take a Ghanaian yes seriously. Ultimately, he understood what I meant: A Ghanaian would hardly say no directly.

In German culture, challenging authority is encouraged, demonstrating confidence and independence. If your upbringing makes challenging authority difficult, it may hinder career progress. Silence in meetings may imply ignorance. In meetings, I've witnessed people confidently discuss trivial matters, creating an impression that their actions will eradicate death!

Ghanaian values of modesty, respect for authority, and humility can be a burden in Germany. I hesitate to ride a bicycle due to a lack of confidence. Although German cities have designated bicycle lanes, some areas require the sharing of roads with vehicles. I feel the bus should have the right of way. Even while walking, I often apologise to those who bump into me. It doesn't mean I'm nicer. I'm not used to bumping into people. If I had grown up experiencing that, I might see it as a normality.

That ends the discussion on some challenges I've faced as a JJC. I guess most of them didn't surprise you. If so, why don't others talk about their experiences? In the next chapter, I'll explain.

9: The conspiracy of silence

From the moment we enter the world, we depend on others. We cry out for attention and care. Even as adults, the need to *be heard* sticks around. We yearn for someone who gets us and listens when we share our fears, dreams, and pains. When you share your story, and someone listens with genuine empathy, it feels like a weight has been lifted. It's like a breath of fresh air, helping you tackle life's challenges. As most football fans will attest, when a referee makes a blunder in the game that costs your team points, hearing former referees and pundits agree that the call was wrong makes the sting slightly less painful, even though the score doesn't change.

Psychologist Carl Rogers discussed the power of nonjudgmental listening. He asserts that sharing your worries with someone who listens without jumping in with their solutions can be incredibly freeing. It's like a burden is lifted, giving you the strength to face your troubles with a fresh perspective. Expressing your thoughts and feelings helps you make sense of your experiences.

On the flip side, bottling up your pain can be harmful. When your feelings are brushed off or invalidated, it can lead to confusion, anxiety, and self-doubt. This kind of manipulation, known as *gaslighting*, messes with your sense of reality and can take a toll on your mental well-being.

When JJCs feel pressured to stay silent about their struggles, it doesn't help them make sense of their journey. Acknowledging these feelings provides a script to cope with the situation. Let's dive into scripts a bit.

A perfunctory offer

In Ghana, when you're eating and someone is nearby, you should tell them, "You're invited," even if they're strangers. If you can't stomach inviting a stranger to join your meal, don't worry; they would typically turn down the offer, although not inviting them might offend. Similarly, if someone invites you to join their meal, take it as a perfunctory offer, which you should decline by saying, "Let it go." What I just described is a Ghanaian script around meals.

Scripts aren't unique to Ghana. They shape our behaviours, expectations, and norms. They influence our daily lives and how we interact with each other. Scripts exist for attending weddings, beaches, or restaurants.

Let us focus on restaurants. The Ghanaian script for going to a restaurant differs from a *chop bar* (an eatery serving affordable food in makeshift structures). Like other places, you usually sit in a restaurant, wait for a server to come to you, place your order, enjoy the meal, and then pay

later. In a *chop bar*, however, you must join a queue at the
stand, place your order (you can even point at the meat you
want), pay on the spot, and carry your food to a table. If you
go to a *chop bar* and wait for a server to take your order, you
might wait forever. Not knowing this script can make you
look awkward.

Scripts aren't the same as societal norms. While norms
represent the broad, often implicit expectations that govern
collective behaviour and values, scripts provide precise,
detailed instructions for how to act or feel in specific
situations. Though scripts usually mirror and adhere to these
broader norms, they extend beyond general influences and
offer concrete guidelines, such as how to greet someone
upon meeting them.

Take, for instance, the Ghanaian cultural demand for
respect for authority. While the norm dictates veneration,
scripts provide how to show this reverence. When meeting a
traditional authority, you might show respect by removing
your footwear and lowering your traditional clothing from
your shoulders. Similarly, when shaking hands with many
people, the script prescribes an anticlockwise motion,
regardless of the seniority of the people you greet.

We learn scripts largely unconsciously, deeply
influenced by our environment. We absorb these scripts
from our families, schools, and social networks. Today, we
can actively seek out and learn scripts from various sources.

Songs, movies, television shows, and social media guide our behaviour in specific contexts. For example, if you have a job interview that includes lunch, YouTube can be a worthy resource for mastering the nuances of cutlery etiquette. Even if you glean no new information from the videos you watch, just knowing that your cutlery skills are already on point can bolster your confidence.

Sometimes, a script can be just knowing the name of a thing, as it is easier to share how you feel if you know the name of that feeling. Consider my example. In July 2019, I was on a flight from Dubai to Munich, seated uncomfortably close to a passenger whose eating habits were, to put it mildly, less than discreet. The cacophony of slurping and chewing from my fellow traveller's seat irritated me. I searched for signs of shared discomfort among my fellow passengers but found none. Then, I began to question whether the problem lay not with the noisy eater but with my own sensitivity.

When I arrived in Munich, I started a quest to uncover the nature of my distress. Through this search, I stumbled upon a term that would bring a hint of order to my inner turmoil: *misophonia*. This word, denoting an intense emotional response to specific sounds such as chewing, slurping, or throat clearing, resonated with my experience. I realised I was not alone in my struggle; others shared this peculiar affliction.

There is no known cure for *misophonia*, but the simple act of finding a name for my discomfort brought with it a measure of solace. Until that point, my suffering had been a silent one, my attempts to communicate my feelings often dismissed as mere fussiness. I wore headsets in public places, a makeshift solution to an issue I couldn't fully explain. But now, armed with a name for my condition, I find a sense of clarity and control. I can tell others about my experience with greater ease and, in doing so, seek understanding and empathy. The act of naming, of finding a script for our feelings, is powerful. It provides us with a framework to understand and express our emotions.

However, not all experiences come with a script. As mentioned earlier, the JJC, struggling to maintain a facade of happiness, has no script. The absence of a script worsens your sense of isolation and uncertainty. Here are some of the reasons JJCs lack a script.

Passing the keys out the window

Do you recall Ezra? Coming from a village, he grappled with the complexities of life at Achimota School. His friends back in the village, perhaps envious of his new life, might have imagined him living a perfect life, far removed from the struggles of their shared past. This envy, in turn, could have exerted a subtle pressure on Ezra, forcing him to project an image of happiness, even when his heart was heavy with unspoken challenges. He also couldn't tell his new peers at Achimota about his issues. Why?

Imagine being in a securely locked house and hearing burglars attempting to break in through the front door. Unless you are on a suicide mission, the last thing you would do is pass your house keys through the window to the thieves. Similarly, Ezra might have kept his issues to himself to shield himself from ridicule.

Throughout history, societies have categorised people into different classes. For instance, in ancient Babylon, Hammurabi's Code established a system dividing people into elites, freemen, and enslaved people. Aristotle also examined class conflicts in his book *Politics*.

Even the English names of some animals and their meat reflect societal hierarchies. The English names for animals often come from Germanic roots, such as pigs, cows, and sheep. On the other hand, the names for the meat come from Norman French or Latin origins, like pork, beef, and mutton. These differences go back to the Norman conquest of England in 1066, where the Normans, who were of French descent, were the ruling class and used French-derived terms for food, while the Anglo-Saxons, the ordinary people, used Germanic terms for the animals.

Despite the lofty ideals outlined in the American Constitution proclaiming equality for all, it also established hierarchies, placing men above women and Whites above others. It is essential to acknowledge that many of the framers of the Constitution were enslavers, leading some to argue that the wealthy American elite crafted the US Constitution to protect their interests.

In Europe, class divisions became more pronounced during the Industrial Revolution. At the bottom of the social ladder were the working class, primarily factory labourers, who lived in dire poverty. Above them were the middle class, people in clerical roles and similar professions. At the pinnacle were the upper class and the super-rich, which included major corporation owners. Sumptuary laws even regulated attire, dictating what people from lower classes could wear and restricting access to certain fabrics or accessories.

Paradoxically, the Industrial Revolution also allowed some ordinary people to amass wealth as the idea of meritocracy gained traction. This concept emphasised that skills and abilities could lead to high-ranking positions despite your background. In Ghana, Osei Kwadwo, the Ashanti King who reigned from 1764 to 1777, implemented a merit-based system for appointing officials, prioritising abilities over birthright.

However, not everyone embraced the idea of ordinary people rising to mingle with the upper class. The rich coned *parvenu* for those who dared to break through the glass ceiling. According to the online version of the *Macmillan*

Dictionary, a parvenu is "someone from a low social class who has become rich or important but is not accepted as an equal by other rich or important people." In ancient Rome, they also used *Novus homo* (new man).

The roots of the term "snobbery" also show how those in privileged positions sought to maintain their superiority and exclude those without aristocratic pedigrees. Philosopher Alan de Botton suggests that the term dates to the 1820s when many Oxford and Cambridge colleges began abbreviating the term *sine nobilitat* – without nobility – to s.nob, written next to the names of students from non-aristocratic homes.

The underlying point here is that those at the top often resist losing or sharing their glory with JJCs, seeking to put them in their place. How often do we see social media posts poking fun at someone struggling to use an escalator upon their arrival in the city? It is common to see people stumble or take missteps, and videos of people grappling with everyday urban tasks, like using cutlery or crossing a busy highway, often circulate with amusement. The joke is always on those from rural areas. We don't mock city slickers who may struggle with tasks associated with village life, such as harvesting ripe papaya. This shows how we make urban scripts the standard and view those who can't meet these standards as needing civilisation.

Thus, if you're Ezra, keeping your challenges to yourself seems wise to save face. Sharing them with those who look down on you would be akin to "handing the keys of the citadel out of the window to the Philistines hammering at the gate." You would not want to arm those with a low opinion of you.

Keeping a coherent picture

If you're a JJC, you may choose not to discuss your struggles to maintain a coherent narrative. We can explain this psychologically. In 1954, a religious sect leader in Chicago claimed that God had revealed to her that He would destroy the world with floods on 21 December 1954. She asserted that since her church members were chosen, God would rescue them from the impending disaster. Fuelled by this belief, some church members made drastic decisions, such as quitting their jobs and selling properties. They fasted, prayed, and awaited the fateful day. But when the day arrived, it passed uneventfully, much like any other day – the sun rose and set.

One might expect the church members to feel upset by the failed prophecy. Strangely, this wasn't the case. Instead of admitting the prediction was false, the members became even more steadfast in their devotion. They believed their fervent prayers and fasting convinced God not to destroy the world.

This unusual response intrigued Leon Festinger and his colleagues, who sought to unravel the mental processes of these steadfast believers. They aimed to understand why, instead of disappointment, their faith increased. Festinger and his team interviewed and experimented with the church members and concluded that humans seek mental consistency and find it unsettling to hold conflicting beliefs, ideas, or values. Festinger termed this discomfort cognitive dissonance.

To lessen cognitive dissonance, we construct narratives that reduce the conflict between our beliefs and the contradictory information we receive. For instance, when we desire something but cannot obtain it, we may adopt a negative attitude toward it, convincing ourselves that we do not want it anyway (*sour grapes*). In the case of the church members, they crafted a new story to reconcile the inconsistency between their beliefs and what they had observed.

Cognitive dissonance applies to various aspects of our lives. If you grew up in a humble cottage on a cocoa farm but managed to achieve success, when sharing your story, admitting to the challenges you meet *after* success can create cognitive dissonance and disrupt the narrative. To keep a consistent and coherent picture, we often disregard elements of our stories that don't fit neatly into our desired narrative. This selective editing serves to ensure harmony and consistency.

If you embody success in your village, you feel compelled to paint a picture of unbound bliss to preserve and enhance this image. You can't afford to admit that you are unhappy. Yet, this distorted picture denies future generations a script and the valuable lessons it could provide for dealing with adversity. The perpetuation of such idealised narratives may lead people to assume that success inevitably leads to happiness.

Shooting the messenger

Another reason JJCs often remain silent about their challenges relates to another human tendency: our natural inclination to hesitate when sharing sad news, known as the minimising unpleasant message (MUM) effect. When others expect us to be happy due to our current status, we often feel compelled to keep our bad news to ourselves. And when we do share it, we may feel the need to sugar-coat it to lessen its impact.

In an experiment, participants were recruited and informed that they were to compare beauty products. The researchers divided the participants into two groups: one received good news, while the other received terrible news. As the participants performed their assigned tasks, they overheard someone mention that they must contact one Glenn Lester at once for either awful or amazing news (depending on their assigned group). Shortly after that, Glenn Lester, one of the researchers, entered the room. The question was whether the participants would tell him what they had heard.

Only two participants from the group who heard the bad news immediately disclosed the complete information to Glenn Lester upon his arrival, whereas nine participants who listened to the good news did so. Curiously, the participants who heard the bad news were more likely to urge Glenn Lester to call home for news without specifying whether it was good or bad, and it took them longer to relay the information. People not only withhold bad news to protect the recipient but also to protect themselves. The tendency to blame the bearer of bad news, known as shooting the messenger, and the fear of others judging you contribute to our reluctance to share bad news.

I recall the time when my sister lost her husband. I had to pick up my nephew and niece from school in another city (Kumasi), and at that point, they were unaware of their father's passing. Upon arriving in Techiman, I took them to their church pastor, hoping he would be the one to inform them. Even the pastor took over an hour to gather the courage to deliver the news, saying their father had *gone to heaven.*

This example shows how deeply ingrained our reluctance to communicate bad news can be, even when we believe it is in the best interest of those affected. The instinct to shield ourselves from blame or negative perceptions can lead us to delay or delegate the task of delivering bad news.

So, I acknowledge that writing this book to disclose bad news is not wise. I understand that discussing my challenges and fears exposes me to potential ridicule. Some people – and I have one in mind – may use this book as evidence to support their claims, saying, "Even he admitted that..." We prefer to share news that enhances our image rather than news that might lead others to think poorly of us. Even when we choose to share negative news, we often sugarcoat it.

Up to this point, I explored why a JJC might opt to keep their struggles private. Yet, we need to acknowledge that JJCs aren't the only ones without a script. Many people can't express their challenges. Let us look at a few of these situations to shed light on the broader effects of this phenomenon.

How to Mourn a Sugar Daddy

On 18 February 2023, rescuers found the body of Ghanaian footballer Christian Atsu under the rubble of his home in Antakya following the dreadful earthquake in Turkey on 6 February 2023. This tragic news brought immense sadness to Ghanaians, as Atsu had played for the national football team, the Black Stars, 65 times. Thus, when a sad husband told his wife of five years about how shattered he felt due to Atsu's death, his wife believed him. Poor her!

It turned out the husband's sadness stemmed from a different reason altogether. The previous day, he had caught his mistress (*side chick,* as Ghanaians call them), for whom he had rented and furnished an apartment, in bed with another man. Crushed with heartbreak, he had no one to share his pain with, certainly not his wife! So, Atsu's death was a perfect opportunity for him to nurse his wounds openly.

I should add that a *side chick* can also find herself in a similar situation. Have you ever seen a mysterious lady at a funeral who wails more intensely than even the widow despite having no clear connection to the deceased? It could be that such a woman had a secret romantic relationship with the deceased while he was alive. Although she also experiences the pain of losing a lover, she lacks a script for mourning. She may not have anyone to console her or understand her anguish. I searched online for *How to grieve a Sugar Daddy* and found no results (Google needs to step up its game!).

Both the man who caught his mistress in bed and the mysterious lady can't disclose the cause of their sorrow, so they must grapple with their pain secretly or find an excuse to cry. In their state of scriptlessness, they don't know how to process their emotions and may resort to strange actions, as shown in a video that went viral on Facebook in 2020. In the video, a heartbroken woman addressed her lover, who had abandoned her.

While the woman wasn't the first victim of a deceitful man, this video stood out. Many of the comments on the video lacked sympathy because, despite being married, she had a boyfriend, and it was the boyfriend who had broken her heart! If you are a married woman, and your boyfriend breaks your heart, how can you cope with the pain? Likely, the lady made the video because she was unsure how to manage her emotions.

The stories of the strange lady at the funeral, the husband betrayed by his *side chick*, and the broken-hearted married woman in the video suggest society denies scripts for behaviours it wishes to discourage. A civilised society can't legislate against every offence. While a society may not outlaw cheating on your spouse, it may discourage such acts.

One way to discourage these deeds is by showing no sympathy to those who engage in them and allowing them to face the outcomes. Ghanaians have even created an acronym for such situations: *wkhkyd.* It means, *Who sent you there?* This phrase reflects the lack of sympathy when you engage in frowned-upon behaviour and suffer negative consequences.

In the Facebook video, if the woman's husband had left her, the comments would've been supportive, and many would've offered support. She could've found comfort in stories and examples highlighting the unfaithfulness of men, which would have aided her in dealing with her pain. They would have assured her that it wasn't her fault, helping her to deal with the pain better.

Yet, society offered little guidance when her boyfriend betrayed her (because she was married). Society, it seems, acts as moral police, denying sympathy for behaviours it looks to discourage. A society may strive to prevent behaviour by providing no scripts for those who suffer from its effects.

The kind stepmother

Sometimes, we don't know how to respond because a situation doesn't fit the usual script; it goes against what we expect. I remember taking my son for a vaccination. After giving the shot, the doctor asked if I was Muslim. That caught me off guard since Germans usually don't bring up religion in casual conversations. When I asked why he was curious, he explained that he wanted to offer my son some candy but wanted to check first because it contained pork. His logic was simple: if I wasn't Muslim, I must eat pork.

I told him I wasn't Muslim but still didn't eat pork. His assumption wasn't entirely wrong – most non-Muslims do eat pork – but it isn't a universal truth. It's the same way we all make quick judgments based on stereotypes. For example, when we hear *stepmother*, many of us automatically think of cruelty. This idea isn't new. Greek myths are full of wicked stepmother stories.

Take Medea, for instance. She married King Aegeus of Athens and had a son, Medus. However, Aegeus already had another son, Theseus, from a past relationship. When Theseus grew up and came to Athens, Medea, fearing he would take the throne from Medus, convinced Aegeus to poison him. Just as Theseus was about to drink, Aegeus recognised him by the sword he carried and knocked the poison away, saving his life.

Stories like this reinforce our biases. Sure, some stepmothers are unkind, but many are loving. The problem is when a step-mum and stepchild don't get along, the default assumption is that the stepmother is at fault. That fits the narrative we expect. On the flip side, if the child is difficult, the stepmother doesn't have a *script* to defend herself. Who would believe her?

Unrequited love

When one person's pain is obvious and the other's isn't, it's easy to overlook both sides of the story. Goethe's *The Sorrows of Young Werther* is a classic example. It paints a heartbreaking picture of unrequited love. Werther falls hard for Charlotte, but she's already engaged. Unable to bear the pain of rejection, he ends his own life, making it easy to see him as the ultimate victim of love that wasn't returned.[2]

---

[2] The story spurred young German men to imitate the character, by copying his dress style and, tragically, his method of dealing

But what about Charlotte's side of things? Imagine someone deeply in love with you, but you just don't feel the same. You try to let them down gently, but that kindness only gives them false hope, making them chase you even more. When you finally make your feelings clear, they're devastated. In extreme cases, they might even threaten to do something drastic, like Werther.

When discussing unrequited love, we almost always focus on the person whose feelings weren't returned. Their heartbreak is obvious, and we naturally sympathize. However, studies show that even when you know you've done the right thing by rejecting someone, it can still leave you feeling guilty. There's no clear roadmap for people in Charlotte's position, leaving them to deal with a mess of emotions on their own.

If you Google *unrequited love*, you'll find tons of results, but nearly all of them focus on the Werthers of the world, not the Charlottes. The ones doing the rejection are often left with guilt and self-doubt, with no real guidance on how to process it. And if their future relationships don't work out, they might even wonder if they made the wrong choice by saying no in the first place.

If those who reject love proposals can experience guilt, you can only imagine the weight of guilt carried by those

---

with unrequited love. This led to the term the *Werther effect*, denoting copycat suicide.

who choose to end a marriage. When you've been married for years, have children together, and decide to pursue a divorce for reasons you consider valid, people may assume that you feel no distress since you're the one initiating the divorce. However, divorce guilt exists. Even with valid reasons, you may still grapple with feelings of guilt, anguish, or grief. You once loved this person (and may still do), and seeing their pain – knowing you're the cause – can leave a bitter taste in the mouth.

Children's presence adds complexity to the decision to part ways. The innocent eyes of your children, who look up to you for stability and love, make severing ties almost awful. The weight of your choice feels enlarged, for it alters your life and that of the children.

In collectivist cultures, extended family members' expectations and pressures intensify your distress. They clamour for the marriage to be preserved, their voices echoing with a mix of concern and tradition. They may plant seeds of doubt in your mind, questioning the certainty of your decision and urging you to consider the impact on your children. These voices are not mere whispers but are fortified by the weight of religious texts and cultural scripts that condemn divorce. As the initiator, you find yourself devoid of such scripts, standing alone in your conviction that divorce, in this instance, is the most humane and rational course of action for all involved.

To understand the pain of someone starting a divorce, we must first recognise how society expects us to honour vows. We're brought up to value promises, which shape how we act in significant ways. When we vow in front of loved ones to cherish someone forever, that promise becomes a heavyweight, symbolised by the marriage certificate. Even if there are solid reasons for divorce, breaking that vow feels like you're letting down not just one person but many. The person initiating the divorce often struggles to justify their decision, haunted by the nagging thought of giving the relationship another shot.

Society rarely offers a pat on the back to move forward, even when it gets the situation. The more pressure you feel to stick with a dysfunctional marriage, the heavier the guilt you carry. This guilt can stick around long after the divorce, as there's no guidebook for the initiator's healing process. How many resources are out there for those starting a divorce? A few blog posts and the occasional YouTube video can't compete with the flood of advice for those on the receiving end.

It takes a lot of guts to start a divorce rather than stay in a loveless relationship. Yet, society often views this bravery with doubt. Meanwhile, those against divorce would be the first to criticise if staying in the union leads to more harm. If you stand your ground and go through with the divorce, people will question your motives. Some might think you're divorcing because you've found someone else. The person you're divorcing might be free to move on, but your actions will be under a microscope. If your ex finds happiness with someone new, they'll get support and understanding. But if you do the same, it'll fuel society's baseless suspicions. In divorce, the initiator often walks a lonely road, finding comfort in believing they're making the best decision for everyone involved.

10: Golden garden with a lead heart

One morning, as King Midas strolled through his palace gardens, he stumbled upon a drunken older man fast asleep in the bushes. Following the Greek tradition of *xenia* (offering hospitality to strangers), Midas took the man in, ensuring he was well cared for. After a few days, the man expressed his wish to return home. Ever the gracious host, Midas escorted him, unaware of who he was.

Upon arriving, the man revealed his true identity. He was Silenus, a companion of Dionysus, the god of wine and celebration. Impressed by Midas's kindness, Dionysus did something rare for a Greek god: he offered Midas any wish he desired. Without much hesitation, the king asked for the ability to turn everything he touched into gold. Dionysus granted his request with a nod.

At first, Midas was thrilled. He imagined a kingdom overflowing with wealth, where everything sparkled with golden brilliance. As soon as he returned to his palace, he eagerly tested his new power. Flowers in his garden turned into solid gold at the slightest touch. Ordinary objects became shimmering treasures. But his excitement quickly turned to horror. When he embraced his wife and daughter, they, too, transformed into lifeless golden statues. Even his loyal dog suffered the same fate.

It was only then that Midas realised the terrible cost of his wish. Trapped in a world of gold, he was utterly alone, with a heart of lead. He couldn't eat or drink; every morsel of food, every drop of water, turned to gold before it could reach his lips. His once-grand palace became a glittering prison.

Today, we often use the phrase *Midas touch* to describe someone with a knack for success. But for the ancient Greeks, Midas's story was a cautionary tale. It reflected a common theme in their mythology: the gods rarely granted gifts without hidden costs. Former boxing champion Mike Tyson summed it up well in an interview: "God punishes you by giving you everything you want just to see if you can handle it."

Midas's story ties into a bigger idea explored in this book: sudden, drastic changes can have unintended consequences. Historian Yuval Noah Harari touches on this in *Sapiens,* exploring the significant revolutions that shaped human history: the cognitive, agricultural, and scientific revolutions. These shifts brought progress, but they also came at a cost.

Take the agricultural revolution, for example. For thousands of years, humans lived as hunter-gatherers, surviving off wild plants and animals. Then, about ten thousand years ago, they started farming by growing crops, domesticating animals, and settling in one place. It seemed like a step forward, offering a more stable food supply. But it also introduced new problems. Farming required backbreaking labour, and while food became more plentiful, diets became less diverse and sometimes less nutritious.

Harari even argues that humans didn't domesticate wheat; wheat domesticated *us*. Once people started farming, they got trapped. They had to care for their crops year-round, stay in one place, and work harder than ever. In this sense, the agricultural revolution was a double-edged sword. This change looked like progress but brought its own set of struggles.

The road not travelled

You can think of class migration in a similar way. Like Midas's golden touch, sudden upward mobility is more of a trap. In the end, Midas begs the wine god to take back his *gift*, finding true relief in the simplicity of his green garden. Should I do the same: leave the city behind and return to the village?

I once encouraged my sister, who still lives in our old farm cottage, to move to the city. Her response caught me off guard: "What would I do there? Here in the village, I have peace of mind. I sleep and wake up whenever I want. What does the city have that I need?" Compared to my daily struggles in the city, her contentment made me wonder who was winning here.

Going back home is tempting, but it's not that simple. There's no guarantee I would find the happiness I'm looking for. Even though life in the city has been tough for me as a JJC, I'm not sure I would trade it for rural life. If I were still working on a cocoa farm, I might be dreaming of my life now, longing for the comforts of the city.

Like I said before, both the village and I have changed. The person I used to be, the home I once knew, are just memories. It's easy to romanticise the road we never took. Discussing the struggles that come with class mobility doesn't mean I would rather be poor. Change is part of life, which helps us move forward, even though it comes at a cost. Medical progress offers an example.

The paradox of progress

Our hunter-gatherer ancestors suffered from diseases that we can now easily cure. We live longer and healthier lives thanks to advances in medicine and technology. We have antibiotics, vaccines, surgeries, and a whole arsenal of drugs that protect us from illnesses that once could wipe out entire populations.

But progress has come with trade-offs. Our diets have changed dramatically. We eat more processed foods, sugar, and unhealthy fats, leading to new health problems like obesity, diabetes, and heart disease. It's odd: modern medicine keeps us alive longer, yet our lifestyle choices create new health risks. Would returning to a hunter-gatherer way of life – eating natural foods and staying active – be the solution? It might seem like it, but it's not that simple when you look at the bigger picture.

Modern medicine exists *because* of the health challenges our lifestyle has created. We tackle problems as they come, just like how scientists developed the COVID-19 vaccine so quickly in response to the pandemic. If we gave up our current way of life to return to foraging, we might also lose the medical advancements that have become essential to our survival. While our diet and lifestyle may introduce new health risks, they've also pushed us to develop treatments that have extended our lifespan. It's a trade-off, and there's no perfect answer. Returning to a simpler life is tempting, but it would likely come at the cost of medical progress and shorter lifespans.

I can speak about the struggles of moving between social classes because I've lived through both the gains and the struggles. But returning to my village wouldn't be as easy as it sounds. I might find it hard to readjust to life there, just as I struggle with the expectations of city life. No matter where we are, we always find something to be dissatisfied with.

Flywheel of society

Instead of going back, I see myself as a trailblazer who connects the scarcity of my past with the opportunities of my present. This role demands sacrifices, like when our ancestors shifted from foraging to farming. I hope to create a foundation for my kids by pushing forward, even when it's tough. As they go to school in Germany, they'll gain the knowledge and middle-class mindset to help them. If they have their own children someday, those kids will benefit even more from the sacrifices made now.

In *Habits*, the philosopher William James argues that habits are like a powerful engine that keeps society running smoothly. They help maintain order and prevent chaos. He adds that habits ensure that people stick to their societal roles, even if they are difficult or unpleasant. Fishermen continue to work at sea during harsh winters, miners stay in dark mines, and farmers remain on their isolated farms throughout snowy months – all because of their habits. That blocks different social classes from mixing too much, keeping people in the social positions they were born into or chose early in life. They make people continue in their chosen paths, even if they aren't ideal, because starting over in a new direction is often seen as too difficult.

So, a JJC breaks away from habit, leaving the position you were born into to a new one. As habits lock us in and make it harder to break, a JJC must be ready to suffer a penalty of mental and cultural disorder. That's why I've decided to accept my trials rather than retreat. Someone must take the first step. The trick now is finding ways to handle the challenges.

Appreciating what I have

One of the ways of dealing with my transition is to come to terms with the fact that things could have been worse, and my life right now is great. I'm trying to control some of our most natural tendencies – like always wanting more – and I've found comfort in the ancient wisdom of *Stoicism.* This philosophy has stood the test of time, offering ways to rein in our endless desires. William Irvine's book, *A Guide to the Good Life*, introduced me to the practical side of Stoicism.

One of its core ideas is that real happiness comes from embracing the present and being content with what we have. It sounds obvious, but we often forget it in the chaos of everyday life. We tend to overlook the very things we once wanted so badly. It's that classic case of not realising what we have until it's gone. The COVID-19 lockdowns were a wake-up call for many of us. Suddenly, even something as simple as a daily walk felt like a privilege.

I have a *Deutschland Ticket*, which lets me travel anywhere in Germany by train. Yet, I haven't left Munich in months. I also have visa-free access to over 170 countries but rarely travel. It's funny. When I didn't have those, I craved them. But once I got them, I moved on to wanting something else. The Stoics understood this pattern well. They taught that we tend to overvalue what we lack, only to take it for granted once we have it. The solution? Practising gratitude and learning to appreciate the present instead of constantly chasing the next thing.

Modern psychology backs this up with the concept of *hedonic adaptation*, the idea that we quickly get used to new things and return to our usual level of happiness. To counter this, the Stoics used a technique called *negative visualization*. This means imagining life without the things we currently have, making us appreciate them more while we still can.

For example, thinking about what life would be like without my job makes me value it more. Reminding myself that I won't have my loved ones forever encourages me to cherish them now. We often think the grass is greener on the other side, but even if it is, we'll probably get used to it and start complaining again. I was excited to come to Germany, but now that I'm here, I catch myself longing for the farm. If I lived there, I would probably watch planes flying overhead and wonder if I would ever get to travel. The truth is, if I have the freedom to fly anywhere today, I should appreciate that.

Another key lesson from Stoicism is knowing what's within our control and what isn't. It's about focusing on what we *can* change and not stressing over what we *can't*. We don't get to choose where we're born or our nurture, but we *can* control how we interpret the past and move forward. Alfred Adler calls this the *separation of tasks*. By focusing on what's in our hands, we can let go of a lot of unnecessary stress.

Seen this way, I see real value in focusing on the journey rather than obsessing over the end goal. I've some control over the process but not the outcome. I've enjoyed writing this book, and whether it succeeds is out of my hands.

I am not that special

Another way I'm learning to deal with my challenges is by reducing the expectations I put on myself. Expectations have a way of shaping how you think, feel, and act. I was reminded of this when my son, who was only eight then, made it vivid. His teacher had asked him to rate himself in different school subjects, and he gave himself lower scores. When I asked why, he admitted he was afraid we might think he was *too* smart. That would mean I would expect too much from him. He didn't want that pressure, so he downplayed his abilities.

His response made me think of a story shared by the French philosopher Michel de Montaigne. He once wrote about a friend who struggled with performance anxiety in intimate situations. To take the pressure off, this friend started openly admitting his fears and limitations to his partners. This honesty gave him a sense of freedom. By lowering expectations, he felt more at ease.

My son's experience and Montaigne's story highlight something interesting: sometimes, we gain confidence by managing the expectations placed on us. When we admit we're not perfect, we set a realistic bar for ourselves and those around us. This way, we're not constantly trying to meet impossible standards.

Being open about my vulnerabilities doesn't mean giving up on growth. It just means acknowledging my limits and understanding that I'm not the centre of the universe. It allows me to build confidence more genuinely.

For me, personal growth isn't about abandoning my identity. It's about learning, adapting, and evolving while staying true to myself (*code-switching*). As a JJC, I know the importance of picking up new skills quickly while keeping my sense of self intact. For example, communication is one skill I'm focusing on. Being able to express myself clearly, whether in speech or writing, is essential for building connections.

That said, I'm careful not to lose myself in the process. I take a balanced approach by gradually exposing myself to new ideas. For example, listening to audiobooks has slowly helped me with pronunciation. This way, I can absorb new skills with less strain. It's about evolving while staying grounded.

No regret-free option

At the end of the day, every choice comes with a cost. Staying true to yourself might mean facing loneliness and discomfort, while constantly code-switching can reinforce impostor syndrome. The right path depends on what you value most. I choose to be myself while adapting my behaviour to suit some contexts. For example, at home, I enjoy some meals with my bare hands, but I won't do that in a corporate setting.

Even there are moments when this *dual identity* proves valuable. Growing up in a rural environment has given me a perspective many city dwellers lack. For instance, I see links between academic theories, Western philosophy, and the wisdom found in Ghanaian proverbs. These proverbs can be hard to grasp for Ghanaians who didn't grow up immersed in them.

The result is two books (in print) – *Botanical Wisdom from West Africa* and *Zoological Wisdom from West Africa* – where I explain Akan proverbs that use plants and animals as metaphors. In these books, I break down their meanings, trace their origins, and connect them to academic and philosophical ideas from different cultures. I couldn't have written them without experiencing both the rural and the urban.

Beyond that, my past has given me resilience, which helps me stay calm in tough situations. Life throws challenges at everyone, but growing up with scarcity has made me more adaptable, more able to endure discomfort without falling apart.

I know that my choice of keeping a dual identity comes with a cost (constantly self-editing is mentally draining). Philosophers have long reflected on the endless choices life presents us. Yet, we only get to live one version of our story. No matter our path, there's always that nagging feeling of *what if?* What if I had chosen differently? Would I be happier? Would life have been better? The Danish philosopher Søren Kierkegaard captured this paradox perfectly in *Either/Or:*

> Marry, and you will regret it; don't marry, you will also regret it; marry or don't marry, you will regret it either way. Laugh at the world's foolishness, you will regret it; weep over it, you will regret that too; laugh at the world's foolishness or weep over it, you will regret both... This, gentlemen, is the essence of all philosophy.

When I look back on my life, it's wild to think about how I went from a quiet village to a busy city life, from working on a farm to diving into intellectual pursuits, and from illiteracy to fully embracing knowledge. I've moved from empty to plenty, and sometimes I wonder what life would've been like if I had stayed in the village. Maybe it would've been peaceful, or perhaps a bit limiting. Either way, I probably would've had regrets. Maybe I would be sitting in that village right now, cursing my bad luck and dreaming of the life I have today. That's why I've decided to live without regrets and accept my path, with all its ups and downs, the joys and the pains.

References

Adam, H., & Galinsky, A. D. (2012). Enclothed cognition. *Journal of Experimental Social Psychology*, 918–925.

Adler, A. (1992). *Understanding human nature.* Oxford: Oneworld Publications.

Agyeman, C., Meeks, K., Beune, E., Owusu-Dabo, E., Addo, J., & Danquah, I. (2016). Obesity and type 2 diabetes in sub-Saharan Africans - Is the burden in today's Africa similar to African migrants in Europe? The RODAM study. *BMC Medicine*, 1-12.

Asch, S. (1956). Studies of independence and conformity: I. A minority of one against a unanimous majority. *Psychological Monographs: General and Applied*, 1-70.

Augsburger, K. (2018, September 11). *Confessions of a Class Migrant.* Retrieved from Medium: https://medium.com/@katie_16182/confessions-of-a-class-migrant-5e7c03c58b25

Ayensu, J., Annan, R., Lutterodt, H., Edusei, A., & Peng, L. S. (2020). Prevalence of anaemia and low intake of dietary nutrients in pregnant women living in rural and urban areas in the Ashanti region of Ghana. *Plos One.*

Baker, D. (1997). Maternal nutrition, fetal nutrition, and disease in later life. *Nutrition*, 807-813.

Baumeister, R. F., Wotman, S. R., & Stillwell, A. M. (1993). Unrequited love: On heartbreak, anger, guilt, scriptlessness, and humiliation. *Journal of Personality and Social Psychology*, 377-394.

BBC News. (2013, April 17). Why people change the way they speak. Retrieved from https://www.bbc.com/news/av/uk-22183566

BBC Sport. (2020, February 26). Alphonso Davies: The Bayern Munich star born in a refugee camp. Retrieved from https://www.bbc.com/sport/football/51644189

Bernstein, P. L. (1996). *Against the Gods - The Remarkable Story of Risk*. New York: John Wiley & Sons Inc.

Berscheid, E., & Reis, H. T. (1998). Attraction and close relationships. In D. Gilbert, S. Fiske, & L. G, *Handbook of social psychology* (4th ed., pp. 193-281). New York: Oxford University Press.

Bierkan, A. T., Sherman, C. P., & Stocquart, E. (1907). Marriage in Roman Law. *The Yale Law Journal, 16*(5), 303-327.

Brehm, J. W. (1966). *A theory of psychological reactance*. New York: Academic Press.

Bundesliga. (2020, December 17). Bayern Munich's Alphonso Davies: "Amazing to be one of the world's best left-backs, but...". Retrieved from https://www.bundesliga.com/en/bundesliga/news/alphonso-davies-amazing-to-be-one-of-the-world-s-best-left-backs-bayern-munich-14017

Burke, E. (1986). *Reflections on the Revolution in France (1790).* Everyman's Library.

Butrimovitz, G. (2000, April-May). Sudden Wealth. *Estate Planning,* p. 41.

Chamorro-Premuzic, T. (2013). Why Do So Many Incompetent Men Become Leaders? *Harvard Business Review.* Retrieved from https://hbr.org/2013/08/why-do-so-many-incompetent-men

Cialdini, R. (1987). *Influence: Science and Practice.* Port Harcourt: A. Michel.

Clance, P. R., & Ament, S. (1978). The imposter phenomenon in high achieving women: Dynamics and therapeutic intervention. *Psychotherapy: Theory, Research and Practice,* 241-247.

Dahik, A., Lovich, D., Kreafle, C., Bailey, A., Kilmann, J., Kennedy, D., . . . Wenstrup, J. (2020). *What 12,000 Employees Have to Say About the Future of Remote Work.* Boston Consulting Group. Retrieved from https://www.bcg.com/publications/2020/valuable-productivity-gains-covid-19

Devitt, P. (2017, May 8). 13 Reasons Why and Suicide Contagion. *Scientific American.*

Edwards, M. (2017). The Barker Hypothesis. In V. Preedy, & V. Patel, *Handbook of Famine, Starvation, and Nutrient Deprivation* (pp. 1-21). Springer.

Festinger, L. (1962). Cognitive Dissonance. *Scientific America,* 93-106.

Finkel, E. J., Hui, C. M., Carswell, K. L., & Larson, G. M. (2014). The Suffocation of Marriage: Climbing Mount Maslow Without Enough Oxygen. *Psychological Inquiry*, 1-41.

Fry, S. (2018). *Heroes: The myths of the Ancient Greek heroes retold.* Michael Joseph.

Fry, S. (2018). *Mythos: The Greek Myths Retold.* Penguin.

Fry, S. (2020). *Troy: Our Greatest Story Retold.* London: Penguin.

Gigerenzer, G. (2014). *Risk Savvy: How to Made Good Decisions.* London: Allen Lane.

Gladwell, M. (2011). *Outliers: The Story of Success.* Back Bay Books.

Gottman, J. M. (1994). *What Predicts Divorce?: The Relationship Between Marital Processes and Marital Outcomes.* New Jersey: Lawrence Erlbaum Associates, Publishers.

Graeber, D. (2018). *Bullshit Jobs: A Theory.* New York: Simon & Schuster.

Grubman, J. (2013). *Strangers in Paradise: How Families Adapt to Wealth Across Generations.* FamilyWealth Consulting.

Gyekye, K. (2011). African Ethics. (E. N. Zalta, Ed.) *The Stanford Encyclopedia of Philosophy.* Retrieved from https://plato.stanford.edu/archives/fall2011/entries/african-ethics/

Han, Y. J., Nunes, J. C., & Drèze, X. (2010). Signaling Status with Luxury Goods: The Role of Brand Prominence. *Journal of Marketing*, 15-30.

Harari, Y. N. (2014). *Sapiens: A brief history of humankind.* Random House.

Hirshman, L. (2006). *Get to Work: A Manifesto for Women of the World.* Viking Adult.

Hofstede, G., Hofstede, G. J., & Minkov, M. (2010). *Cultures and Organisations: Software of the Mind.* New York City: McGraw Hill Education Ltd.

Ingram, P., & Oh, J. J. (2022). Mapping the Class Ceiling: The Social Class Disadvantage for Attaining Management Positions. *Academy of Management Discoveries, 8*(1).

James, W. (1914). *Habit.* New York: Henry Holt and Company.

Kahneman, D. (2011). *Thinking, Fast and Slow.* New York: Farrar, Straus and Giroux.

Klarman, M. J. (2016). *The Framers' Coup: The Making of the United States Constitution.* Oxford University Press.

Kraus, M., Côté, S., & Keltner, D. (2010). Social Class, Contextualism, and Empathic Accuracy. *Psychological Science, 21*(11), 1716-1723.

Lorenzen, J. A. (2007). Diderot effect. *The Blackwell Encyclopedia of Sociology.*

Lyons-Padilla, S., Gelfand, M., Mirahmadi, H., Farooq, M., & van Egmond, M. (2015). Belonging Nowhere: Marginalization and Radicalization Risk Among Muslim Immigrants. *Behavioral Science & Policy, 1*(2), 1-12.

MacCurdy, J. T. (1943). *The Structure of Morale.* Cambridge: Cambridge University Press.

MacFarlane, C., & Haweis, H. R. (1880). *Life of Napoleon Bonaparte.* New York: George Routledge and Sons.

Macmillan Dictionary. (n.d.). Parvenu. Retrieved from https://www.macmillandictionary.com/dictionary/british/parvenu

Mahama, J. D. (2012). *My First Coup D'etat: And Other True Stories from the Lost Decades of Africa.* New York City: Bloomsbury.

Martin, S., Côté, S., & Woodruff, T. (2016). Echoes of Our Upbringing: How Growing Up Wealthy or Poor Relates to Narcissism, Leader Behavior and Leader Effectiveness. *Academy of Management Journal*, 2157-2177.

Maslow, A. (1943). A theory of human motivation. *Psychological Review, 50*(4), 370-396.

Milgram, S. (1963). Behavioral Study of obedience. *The Journal of Abnormal and Social Psychology*, 371–378.

Miller, D. (1990). *Icarus Paradox.* New York: HarperBusiness.

Moriarty, T. (1975). Crime, commitment, and the responsive bystander: Two field experiments. *Journal of Personality and Social Psychology*, 370-376.

Morley, K. (2022). *Beat Gender Bias: How to play a better part in a more inclusive world.* Elsternwick: Major Street Publishing.

Nilles, B. (2019, January 9). *Public Meltdowns, Family Cash Grabs and a Life-Changing Diagnosis...* Retrieved from Eononline: https://www.eonline.com/news/1003208/public-meltdowns-family-cash-grabs-and-a-life-changing-diagnosis-inside-susan-boyle-s-fight-against-the-pitfalls-of-sudden-fame

Raghunathan, R. (2016). *If You're So Smart, Why Aren't You Happy?* Portfolio.

Rankin, C. H., Abrams, T., Barry, R. J., Bhatnagar, S., Clayton, D. F., Colombo, J., . . . McSweeney, F. K. (2009). Habituation revisited: an updated and revised description of the behavioral characteristics of habituation. *Neurobiology of learning and memory*, 135-138.

Rebeiro, A. (2003). *Dress and Morality.* Berg Publishers.

Rodgers, C. (1980). *A Way of Being.* Boston: Houston Mifflin Company.

Rosen, S., & Tesser, A. (1970). On Reluctance to Communicate Undesirable Information: The MUM Effect. *Sociometry, 33*(3), 253-263.

Rutledge, P. (2011, November 8). Social Networks: What Maslow Misses. *Psychology Today*. Retrieved from https://www.psychologytoday.com/intl/blog/positively-media/201111/social-networks-what-maslow-misses-0

Shillington, K. (1995 (1989)). *History of Africa.* New York: St. Martin's Press.

Silvermint, D. (2018). Passing as privileged. *Ergo*, 1-43.

Stadler, M. (1989). On learning complex procedural knowledge. *Journal of Experimental Psychology: Learning, Memory, and Cognition*, 1061–1069.

Streib, J. (2015). *Power of the Past.* Oxford University Press.

The Fawcett Society. (2022). *Broken ladders: the myth of meritocracy for women of colour in the workplace.* Retrieved from https://www.fawcettsociety.org.uk/Handlers/Download.ashx?IDMF=72040c36-8cd6-4ae3-93f3-e2ad63a4b4b0

The Mail on Sunday. (2022, February 5). 'I would lock myself away and drink for two days... the anger would build up to an explosion'... Retrieved from https://www.dailymail.co.uk/sport/football/article-10479635/Wayne-Rooney-battled-inner-rage-demons-Manchester-United-England-career.html

The New York Time. (1864, April 28). The Moral Police of Society. *The New York Times*, p. 4. Retrieved from https://www.nytimes.com/1864/04/28/archives/the-moral-police-of-society.html

Tomkins, S. (1987). Script Theory. In J. Arnoff, A. I. Rabin, & R. Zucker, *The Emergence of Personality* (pp. 147–216). New York: Springer Publishing Company.

Utley, I. (2016). *Culture Smart! Ghana.* London: Kuperard.

Vance, J. D. (2016). *Hillbilly Elegy: A Memoir of a Family and Culture in Crisis.* New York: Harper Press.

Williams, J., Multhaup, M., & Mihaylo, S. (2018). Why Companies Should Add Class to Their Diversity Discussions. *Harvard Business Review.* Retrieved from https://hbr.org/2018/09/why-companies-should-add-class-to-their-diversity-discussions

Wrede, I. (2022, May 31). Social class: Germany's forgotten career hurdle. Retrieved from https://www.dw.com/en/social-class-germanys-forgotten-career-hurdle/a-61978626

Acknowledgements

To Dr. Gifty Baffour Awuah, I extend my deepest gratitude. You encouraged me to translate thoughts into words. Our many talks while I ambled through the book's themes have been invaluable. Your insightful feedback has been a beacon, guiding this project to fruition.

I am equally indebted to friends whose support I could count on throughout this journey. Dr. Stephen Asabere, Imke Horten, Tlaagatso Nemasasi, Nana Afua Opokuaa, and Joachim Schroeter. Your readiness to read the manuscript and offer your thoughts has enriched this work hugely.

My mother, Auntie Maggie, stands out for her relentless dedication to my education. My sister Martha and her late husband, K. Ahimah, have been pillars of support. To K. Acheampong, Jeff T. Ampofo, Augustus Eghan, and Simone Ruiz-Vergote, your presence has been incredibly impactful, and for that, I am grateful.

Finally, my gratitude goes to Awurama, Nana Ama, and Kofi. Your interest and persistent questions about the book inspired me. Thank you for being the light that shaped the essence of this book, *my descendants.*

Made in the USA
Columbia, SC
28 April 2025

57272247R00090